Growing Old-fashioned Flowers

A Warwickshire cottage garden with spring flowers

Growing
Old-fashioned Flowers

Roy Genders

with four colour plates by
Mary McMurtrie

David & Charles
Newton Abbot London Vancouver

To my son Robert
who shares my love
of the old-fashioned flowers

ISBN 0 7153 6873 7

© Roy Genders 1975

Set in 10 on 12 point Plantin
and printed in Great Britain
by Morrison & Gibb Limited,
London and Edinburgh
for David & Charles (Holdings) Limited
South Devon House Newton Abbot Devon

Published in the United States of America
by David & Charles Inc
North Pomfret Vermont 05053 USA

Published in Canada
by Douglas David & Charles Limited
132 Philip Avenue North Vancouver BC

Contents

List of Illustrations

Colour

Monotone

All photographs by John Gledhill except where credited.

Collecting and Enjoying Old-fashioned Flowers

The old-fashioned flowers, favourites of our gardens until a few years ago, have now almost vanished and we miss them greatly. Though hardy, these plants demand some time, care and attention in their propagating. Today, the nurseryman, with the high cost of labour, must do all he can to eliminate his overheads, with the consequence that the plants of cottage gardens are absent from all but a few specialist catalogues.

Less than a decade ago, that velvety crimson primrose, 'Miss Massey', could be bought from a nursery in the northwest for a pound a sackful. Now the land is built on and I do not know a single garden where this flower may be found. Similarly, the double white primrose could, at one time, be bought for a few pence a root. It can still be obtained, but becomes scarcer each year and its price is now much higher. The scented 'Marie Crousse' with its huge purple flowers flecked with white, a strong and vigorous grower in all types of soil, has become almost as scarce and many collectors would give several pounds a plant for 'Rose du Barri' and 'Bon Accord Purity' were they available.

In short, the old-fashioned plants are now collector's items in the same way as coins, stamps and cigarette cards. Those which were once discarded with little respect have now come to be worth our attention. Almost any price can be obtained for violets believed to be extinct and for those carnations and pinks mentioned by Chaucer and Milton. Yet it is rare that a flower vanishes entirely from cultivation and somewhere, in a cottage garden, however remote, a few plants will still exist. Such plants are well worth saving as they have a charm and character of their own, but it is on the energies of a few enthusiasts that the survival of old varieties now depends.

Building a Collection

Yet every amateur gardener with time to spare to look around can grow these 'rare' plants. It is possible to build up a general collection or to specialise in one or two which are best suited to the conditions of your garden or which give the most pleasure. But, whichever plants are decided upon, you will have to search for them, a pastime which greatly adds interest to the collection. It is of little use simply reading through advertisements in the daily newspapers or the catalogues of most nurserymen for most likely these will contain no mention of such flowers.

Those who live near a village will be best situated to start a collection for in most cottage gardens there may still grow at least a few of the old-fashioned plants. Mention to friends that you are searching for a particular variety of plant and they, in turn, will ask others. It is surprising how, in this way, many will come to light. Those who are motorists should stop in any village and take a leisurely walk, looking in every garden to see if there still grows any of the plants that are sought. More than likely the cottager will be only too pleased to part with or exchange a few roots. I once had the good fortune to be in a village where, in a tiny cottage garden, grew masses of the double primrose, 'Rose du Barri', with its huge blooms of a lovely shade of deepest pink. As it was long since believed to be extinct, my delight at finding this beauty can well be imagined and I could not resist the temptation to knock on the door. The householder, in his eighties, told me that he was born in the cottage and knew that the plants were well established when he was a child. There they must have been growing, like weeds, for more than a century. He was pleased to dig up several large clumps for me to take away to build up a stock.

In searching for old plants, one should remember that they are to be found mostly in the areas in which they were originally grown. The finest exhibition pansies and violas have always been grown in the cold, moist regions of the northern Midlands and northwest England and today, at the great summer shows, the last of the specialist growers and exhibitors of these lovely flowers all seem to come from those areas. The south is too warm and eastern England is too dry for the plants to do well.

For the same reason, many old primroses are to be found in Ireland and in the western regions of the UK where the climate is mild but moist. Pinks, on the other hand, love the dryness and sunshine and grow best down the eastern side and along the south coast. Like lavender, they prefer an open position and a gravelly, chalky soil, the very opposite to primroses and pansies with their liking for shade and a moist peaty soil. Conditions of soil and climate where plants are to be found will indicate if a particular plant is suitable for your own garden.

Old-fashioned Flowers in the Modern Garden

Some gardeners may aim generally at re-creating the atmosphere of an old-world garden with cottage garden flowers; others may have more specific objectives such as to make a Shakespeare garden, planting those old-fashioned flowers mentioned in the plays, or a garden of love, including all those flowers used in lover's posies or as charms. A garden may be made with those plants which have Biblical connections such as St John's Wort, the Christmas Rose and the double form of Our Lady's Smock. All these plants may still be found in cottage gardens and are listed for the time being at least in a few nurserymen's catalogues.

Herbaceous border in a small garden with pinks, lupins and delphiniums

The lovely old plants, so many with delicious perfume, are right to use in every garden whether in town or country. Something of the old-world atmosphere may be created by dividing the gardens into a number of smaller gardens, by means of brick or stone walls or by planting hedges of beech or hornbeam and leaving a 3ft wide gap through which one may enter. Even where there is no garden, but only a paved courtyard, the flowers may be grown in tubs, the oak casks of West Country cider makers being admirable for the purpose. So that surplus moisture may drain away, holes should be drilled in the base and the tubs should be placed on bricks or stones to ensure a free circulation of air around them.

A small piece of garden may be divided into small beds by using crazy paving stone or those plants of neat tufted habit may be confined to the area of soil surrounded by the iron or wooden rim of an old cart wheel. If the spokes are still there, press the wheel into the soil and set out the plants in each section, one variety to each. Alternatively edge the beds with a dwarf lavender or with cotton lavender (*santolina*) planted 15in apart and keeping it clipped to no more than 15ins high. Or plant in an orchard kept clear of grass. Here, most of the old-fashioned flowers will flourish in the dappled shade of standard apple and pear trees. The same trees may be used at the back of a border where, to the front, may be planted paeonies and all those other hardy cottage garden flowers which will revel in the shade of the trees as they reach maturity.

Almost all the old-fashioned flowers love a soil containing decayed manure and some humus. This may be given in the form of peat or leaf mould or use the clearings from ditches if you live in the country, whilst decayed material from the garden compost heap should be worked into the soil whenever possible. One of the secrets of growing and maintaining the old plants in healthy condition was to provide them with plenty of humus which nurtured the young roots which form at the crown of the plants and hold moisture so that artificial watering was almost unnecessary. Watering with a powerful jet will wash the soil from the plants and leave them impoverished, whilst the continual use of the hose will wash the valuable trace elements from the soil. The plants will greatly benefit from a yearly mulch of sifted loam and peat to which has been incorporated a little decayed manure or used hops. This should be given in spring, before the ground becomes dry and parched, and should be worked with the fingers right up to the crown of the plant. They will reward this additional care in their culture by remaining healthy and vigorous through the years whilst they will bear a quantity of bloom undreamed of from plants growing in a dry, half-starved soil.

Cultural Needs

A greenhouse will not be necessary for growing the old plants for they are all hardy and are mostly propagated by root division, re-planting to the open ground into beds of prepared soil.

For those growing pansies and violas, a simple frame will be valuable in which to strike the cuttings and here, too, cuttings (or pipings as they are more correctly called) of pinks and carnations will be inserted.

A frame may be constructed from old railway sleepers, though these now have an antique value and may be difficult to find. A frame may also be constructed from three rows of bricks held together by cement with the first row set into a cement base. Or use two widths of floor boarding, cut to the dimensions of the frame light and held together by short pieces of 1in timber. Strong stakes driven into the ground will hold the sides in place.

The lights may be obtained already made up and will usually be $4\frac{1}{2}$ft × $3\frac{1}{2}$ft. Larger lights as used by nurserymen should not be used as they are heavy to move when watering and ventilating. Lights of simple construction may be made from lengths of 2in wide timber and with cross pieces at regular intervals, whilst transparent plastic sheeting may be used instead of glass. The frame would be inexpensive to make and be light to handle but in windy weather it should be held in place by stretching across it two lengths of plastic-covered wire fastened to the sides or pegged to the ground.

Where timber is used for the frame, make sure that it has been treated with a reliable wood preservative before using it. Obtain new timber if possible for old wood may be affected by pest and disease. The sides of the frame should be no more than 12in deep and may be only about 8in deep so that the cuttings, as they root, will not be too far from the glass or polythene.

During warm, sunny weather, it will be necessary to shield the cuttings from the direct rays of the sun and this is done by whitening the underside of the glass or using a frame blind.

All types of cuttings will root more quickly in a compost of sand and peat in equal parts by bulk. Both will be virtually sterile and so be free of pest and disease. The cuttings will love to feel the grit which encourages rapid rooting (in the same way that geraniums root better around the sides of an earthenware pot) whilst the peat will help to retain moisture. Put in the compost to a depth of 3in and before watering, make the surface level and the compost gently firm. Most cuttings are inserted 2–3in apart and made comfortably firm. They are then watered in and the frame light put in position. Ventilation should not be necessary until the cuttings begin to root but regular syringing with clean water, two or three times daily in warm weather, will prevent the cuttings from 'flagging' for there will be only limited loss of moisture.

When rooted, pansies and pinks may be grown on in small pots containing the John Innes potting compost obtainable from most garden shops or they may be sold simply as rooted cuttings, planting a number as stock plants from which to take cuttings in the future. Or make up a potting compost from sifted turf loam (3 parts or half by bulk) and 1 part each peat, coarse sand and decayed manure. Mix well together and do not use old garden soil which will be full of weed seeds.

If growing for sale, it will be quite easy to dispose of the plants locally for gardeners are always on the look out for something choice and different. In addition, try inserting an advertisement in the local paper or in the national garden weeklies and the Saturday newspapers which usually contain a gardening section on that day. Often just one order for plants will cover the cost of the insertion. When mailing the plants wrap them carefully in damp moss or some other moisture-holding material and pack firmly in a box which is not too large so that they will not shake about. Do not omit to name the plants for varieties without a name have little value to collectors as with water colours or oil paintings. And remember to post off the plants early in the week so that they will reach their destination before the weekend and not be too long confined to the containers. Most people garden at the weekends and plants arriving late may be left without attention for another week.

It is possible to build up a collection of several different types of plant before dealing in them but usually a comprehensive collection of just one, maybe with another closely related plant such as primroses and auriculas together, will enable you to concentrate on their cultural requirements and perhaps have printed a catalogue of varieties. Catalogues are kept for a long time and enable enthusiasts to order from them over an extended period, even though prices may have increased. This can be adjusted later. Remember to add postage costs to each order for these can be considerable.

An additional interest to be gained from the old flowers is that most of them attract considerable attention on the show bench where there are special classes for most of them. There is great joy to be had from winning an award with a flower which *you* have grown, and showing will also build up a reputation as a specialist grower of a particular plant.

And a final point in the favour of almost all the old-fashioned flowers is that they are ideally suited to the small modern garden, requiring no staking, and are extremely durable. The original outlay will possibly be the last for any particular variety. Some plants growing in my garden were obtained forty years ago, during which time they have been divided into hundreds of offsets, and still they continue to multiply and bear a profusion of bloom.

Primroses

*'The peering primrose, like a sudden gladness
Gleams on the soul.'*

SAMUEL TAYLOR COLERIDGE

Of all our native flowers the primrose is perhaps the best loved, possibly because it is one of the earliest to bloom or because of the ethereal moonlight yellow of its flowers. Those primroses found so commonly in the gardens of cottage and manor in Tudor days are outstanding collector's plants, partly because of their complete hardiness and partly because they are eminently suited to the small garden, the rockery and the window-box.

The plant takes its name from primaverola, a diminutive of *prima vera*, meaning the first flower of springtime. It developed into primerole, and one of the earliest writings to mention this name was that of Walter de Biblesworth in the late thirteenth century:

> Primerole et primeveyre
> Sur tere aperunt entems de veyre

The name soon became 'primrose' which, in Shakespeare's time, was a plant held in so great esteem as to be the word most often used to denote excellence, as when Spenser wrote 'She is the pride and primrose of the rest'.

It was during the reigns of the Tudors that primroses first came to be widely grown for the beauty and interest of their flowers, for by then many variations of the wild primrose had become known. Tabernaemontanus, writing in 1500, described the double yellow primrose which may still be found in its double form growing wild in various parts of the country. Variations of *Primula acaulis* or *P. vulgaris*, are extremely numerous and, quite apart from the double forms, there are the dainty Hose-in-Hose forms and the Jack-in-the-Greens. By Elizabethan times, these primroses were widely grown in the gardens of both manor house and cottage, for besides being of perennial habit, the compact form of the plants made them ideal for this form of gardening.

Though the different forms of the white and yellow primrose must have been well known since earliest times, they had not been mentioned in any detail until the works of Gerard and Parkinson appeared during the last years of the sixteenth century and the beginning of the seventeenth century. John Gerard, though not a gardener by profession, looked after Lord Burghley's garden in London and eventually had an equally famous garden of his own. In his *Herbal*, he described and illustrated the double white primrose (*alba plena*) and also a number of other forms, especially the Jack-in-the-Green

The single blooms backed with ruff-like miniature leaves of the Jack-in-the-Green primrose

Looking 'like the breeches men do wear', the Hose-in-Hose primrose

primroses. Here, the blooms are single, backed by a ruff-like arrangement composed of tiny replicas of the primrose leaf, which provides a pleasing contrast to the clear colourings of the blooms. They were widely planted during the sixteenth century and plants later became known as Jack-in-the-Pulpits.

An interesting form of the Jack-in-the-Green is the Jack-a-napes-on-Horseback. This is the Franticke or 'Foolish' primrose (or cowslip) described so well by Parkinson in his *Paradisus* of 1629: 'It is called Foolish because it beareth at the top of the stalk a tuft of small, long, green leaves with some yellow leaves, as it were pieces of flowers broken and standing amongst the green leaves'. A plant of polyanthus form it is shown in the *Paradisus*, the leaves being further apart and not held in close circular formation as for the Jack-in-the-Green. The striping of the leaves is of the same colouring as the bloom. Gerard's Jack-a-napes shows a larger flower which sits on a saucer of the same colour, striped with green. It possibly takes its name from a striped coat which was fashionable during the seventeenth century. A book of early Stuart times described the flower as being 'all green and jagged', whilst Gerard says that it is so named by the women, 'the flowers being wrinkled and curled after a most strange manner'. I have yet to understand where 'the Horseback' part comes in. Most of the old Jacks during recent years have been rediscovered in Ireland where the mild, moist climate is so suited to primrose culture and where many parts have been undisturbed for centuries.

The Gally Gaskin form of primrose is a single bloom which has a swollen, distorted calyx and is now rarely to be found. It also has a frilled ruff beneath the bloom. A picture attributed to Henri Coiffier de Ruse in the National Gallery, London, aptly illustrates this flower, a frilled ruff appearing beneath the knees of the gentlemen which appear large, like the swollen calyx of the Gally Gaskin.

Perhaps the loveliest of all primrose forms is that of the Hose-in-Hose, where one bloom grows from another to give a plant in full bloom a dainty, feathery appearance. They are also known as Duplex, Double-decker or Cup and Saucer primroses. Parkinson wrote: 'They remind one of breeches men do wear'. Indeed, the hose worn by men at that time were knitted with a much stronger wool than used today and it was the custom for one stocking to be placed in another before being passed to the wearer, just like the flowers. The botanical explanation of this effect is that the lower 'bloom' is really a petaloid calyx. In one variation to the Hose-in-Hose form the calyx of the lower flower is striped with green, red or yellow. This has given rise to the name Pantaloon to describe a flower which is perhaps more unusual than pretty.

Value in the Garden

Their ability to flower to perfection under all conditions adds to the popularity of the primrose. Nor is there any lovelier sight in spring than a few of the sweetly scented, deep purple 'Marie Crousse', introduced from France a century ago, planted with our native primrose. 'Red Paddy' from Ireland, the dainty orange-red flowers edged with silver is also charming to edge a small path, whilst planted amongst a bed of daffodils, especially the pure white trumpeted varieties, the old Cornish primrose 'Tyrian Purple' looks supreme.

For spring bedding the *Juliae* forms are amongst the best of all hardy plants and should always be grown where cold wind and heavy snow are likely to cause damage to wallflower plants. The hardiness of the primrose and its ability to overcome adverse conditions may be given in the following example. When we moved from one home to another during early autumn, it was necessary to store several thousand plants together with the furniture. The primroses were lifted in a reasonably moist condition and placed for storage in large wooden tea-chests. As we were unable to take over the new property for fully two months, the plants remained in store for that length of time. They were planted in nursery beds in early November and the following spring gave a magnificent display with less than one per cent loss.

Most of the *Juliae* primroses are excellent plants for using as a ground cover for tulips, those which bloom early, such as *Altaica grandiflora*, 'Mauve Queen' and the deep purple flowered 'Fruhlingzauber' providing a pleasing contrast to the tulips. These early flowering primroses will come into bloom before the end of March and, by planting a number of varieties, bloom may be enjoyed until the end of May in the North where the plants appreciate the cool conditions. With their ability to transplant readily, several large clumps may be lifted about the beginning of March, as soon as the ground is clear of frost, and may be planted in shallow bowls to be taken indoors.

Those which bloom on long stems, like 'Mauve Queen' and 'Spring Charm', look good in posie bowls, whilst those of polyanthus habit, bearing a number of blooms from the end of a sturdy main stem, are also delightful in small vases. Several varieties have a more pronounced polyanthus habit and may even be described as being miniature polyanthuses. Into this category comes 'Barrowby Gem' and 'Lady Greer'.

Culture

Being rather less robust, the double primroses are best lifted and divided between early July and late in September which will allow them to become well established before winter. Early August is perhaps the best time, being generally a period of rainy weather, for all primroses must have moisture to become established or they will die. The tougher *Juliae* hybrids and other forms of the primrose may be lifted and divided at almost any time when the soil is moist and friable. July is a suitable month or any time between early October and early March. The primrose is able to withstand transplanting when in bloom better than almost any other plant, for if the plants are lifted with plenty of soil they will quickly re-establish themselves and will continue to bloom quite oblivious of such a move. They must, of course, be kept moist until re-established. However, in certain parts, spring is often a time of strong drying winds, and along the eastern side of Britain it is advisable to plant late in autumn or early winter. Then the plants will give a brilliant display the following spring, irrespective of the weather.

The deeply veined leaf of the primrose enables it to direct the least drop of moisture falling on its surface to the crown of the plant. Thus it has been endowed by nature to survive dry conditions if they do not continue for too long a time.

When planting, set quite deeply and make very firm by treading if the soil is friable. The most robust of the *Juliae* primroses should be planted 12in apart, whilst the doubles and those of more compact habit may be planted 8in apart. Of those of neat habit, suitable for window box, trough and the small rockery, the salmon-flowered 'E. R. James', the white 'Snow Cushion' and 'Rubin', with its burgundy-red blooms, are outstanding, making almost no foliage when they come into bloom, the plants being covered with stemless flowers 1in (2½cm) in diameter.

The demise of the double primroses must be due chiefly to the advent of the motor car and the rise of industry, resulting in a shortage of humus for our gardens. Double primroses will not thrive without humus, even if it be a substitute for farmyard manure which they appreciate so much. Horticultural peat is of the greatest value for working into the soil, so are spent hops and,

The old double white primrose, *Alba plena*

of course, leaf mould. Dried and chopped pea and bean haulm will provide valuable nitrogen as will seaweed. Not only must a quantity of humus be well worked in at planting time but it must be remembered that primroses form their new roots at, or just above, soil level, the old root stock gradually falling into decay and playing no part in the future life of the plant. This makes an annual top dressing or mulch with peat or leaf mould essential in maintaining their vigour.

It is often said that the double primroses are not easily grown, yet I find that a rooted division soon makes a large plant, covering itself in a mass of bloom from March until May. Many of them bloom again in late autumn and several, such as 'Our Pat', will continue to bear odd blooms through the winter months.

No frame is needed to propagate members of the primrose family. Each plant will, after twelve months, have formed a number of offsets which may be divided by 'teasing' them apart. The roots should never be cut into pieces or bits may come apart without any roots. It will, however, be possible to remove an offset from an established plant without its being lifted by means of a little, small-nosed trowel.

Where it is desired to obtain as many varieties as possible, they may be planted in groups of half a dozen or so in almost any corner of the garden, and they will always be happiest in partial shade, where the spring sunshine does not fade the bloom nor the summer sun dry out the soil. With their liking for some shade they may be planted where most other plants would not flourish.

So that the spring display does not suffer unduly, it will be advisable to lift and divide several clumps each year so that a number will bear a profusion of bloom and can be divided after flowering. The offsets may also be set out in rows in small beds and sold or exchanged as required. Primroses are amongst the easiest plants to transport, most of the soil being shaken from the fleshy fibrous roots which should be tied separately or in bundles, damp moss being placed around the roots. They may be packed in boxes tightly together to prevent them from being unduly shaken about. Wherever possible, the plants should be lifted only when the ground is moist.

Double Primrose Varieties

ARTHUR DU MOULIN A bright, clear violet colour. This is one of the few doubles to set seed, really being semi-double.

BON ACCORD BEAUTY An outstanding flower, the claret-red blooms being edged with white.

BON ACCORD CERISE The blooms have a flat appearance and are a cerise-pink shade.

BON ACCORD GEM Has rosy-mauve petals, attractively waved.

BON ACCORD LAVENDER Quite large blooms with frilled petals, of a rich shade of lavender-mauve.

BON ACCORD LILAC   Bears a dainty flat bloom of shell-pink flushed with lilac and with a yellow centre.

BON ACCORD PURITY   One of the loveliest varieties, the blooms being rounded and of pure icy-white with a green centre and held upright on strong stems.

BON ACCORD PURPLE   The symmetrical blooms are of deepest purple, flushed with crimson. Of semi-polyanthus habit.

CHEVITHORNE PINK   Its beautiful orchid-pink blooms are held on a sturdy main stem.

CLOTH OF GOLD   A really lovely variety, the fully double rounded blooms being of a rich shade of creamy-yellow.

CRATHES CRIMSON   Bears fragrant pink blooms, flushed with crimson.

CRIMSON KING   Large blooms of a rich shade of crimson-red. Of vigorous, sturdy habit.

DOWNSHILL ENSIGN   The deep purple blooms are of a shaggy appearance and borne on long footstalks from a polyanthus stem.

MARIE CROUSSE   An old French variety bearing huge blooms of royal purple edged and marked with white.

MARINE BLUE   The small, dainty blooms are of clear mid-blue shaded red at the centre.

OLD ROSE   The large fully double blooms are rose-pink. Of strong constitution.

OUR PAT   Has a sturdy constitution with bronzy-green foliage and bears a profusion of small amethyst-blue flowers.

QUAKER'S BONNET   The blooms are of unusual shape with a high centre and are lilac-mauve.

RED PADDY   Bears a tiny, fragrant symmetrical bloom of orange-red edged with silver.

TYRIAN PURPLE   Possibly the finest of all the doubles, bearing large royal purple blooms, flushed with red.

WILLIAM CHALMERS   Raised in Scotland, this is a sturdy grower. The large well-formed blooms are of midnight blue, flushed with purple.

Juliae Hybrids

AFTERGLOW   Originating in the west of England, this is a superb new primrose, of rich rust-orange colour with a distinct eye. It has a long flowering season.

ALTAICA GRANDIFLORA   An old variety (from the Caucasus), but none the less attractive. Early to bloom, the flowers are of a pure mauve-pink of real primrose habit, and most prolific.

AVALON   Enjoys shade, and when first seen was thought to be a bed of 'Princess of Wales' violets, with which it is almost identical in its violet-blue colouring. A new primrose, remaining in bloom for a very long period and very prolific indeed. Makes a lovely house plant in glass bowls in early April.

BETTY GREEN   A new Dutch variety having vivid claret-red blooms of medium size, very freely produced, and attractive rich apple-green foliage.

BLUE HORIZON   Of neat, compact habit and bearing flowers of clear sky blue.

CHARLES BLOOM   Blooms are a rich shade of velvety crimson-purple with an orange eye.

CRADDOCK'S WHITE It has dark bronzy foliage and bears a pure white bloom. Plant with a red-flowering variety.

CRIMSON GLORY   New and wonderful, it is of polyanthus formation with the huge individual blooms of a rich crimson-red.

DAVID GREEN   Should be in every collection. The dark burgundy-red blooms are very free and, against the vivid emerald-green foliage, with the evening sun behind, make a plant that is outstandingly beautiful. A bloom with almost complete lack of eye.

DINAH   A gem from Holland, remaining eight weeks in bloom. The dainty blooms are like velvet, burgundy-crimson in colour, and have a unique olive-green eye. In bloom again in late autumn when it is more colourful than any primrose.

E. R. JANES   A grand trough garden primrose with small crinkled pale green foliage and bears masses of orange-pink flowers over a long period.

FAIR MAID   From Scotland, very late, but outstanding in every way. Of miniature polyanthus habit the blooms are of a rich vermilion-rust with a unique double yellow eye. The sturdy bronze stems make it a grand cut flower and most suitable for window box cultivation.

F. ASHBY   The most dwarf and unusual *Juliae* primrose, having almost black foliage and bearing a dark crimson bloom.

FRUHLINGZAUBER   A beauty, bearing its large flat blooms of royal-purple above brilliant green foliage.

GARRYARDE primroses   First discovered in Ireland, this race has almost black bronzy foliage which is a striking contrast to the paler leaved varieties as well as to their bloom. The following have the unique 'Garryarde' foliage:

Buckland Primrose   The blooms are of a rich Jersey cream colour and long lasting.

Canterbury   A new variety of outstanding beauty, the large flat blooms being of deep cream flushed with apricot.

Dr Molly   Crimson blooms, with darkest bottle green foliage.

Guinevere   The bloom is of a pastel pink shade with a yellow eye.

The Grail   One of the best in this group, the bloom being of Elizabethan brick-red.

Victory   It has less bronzy leaves than the others and bears a bloom of paeony-purple.

GLORIA   Glowing crimson-red flowers on long sturdy stems. The petals have a distinct white vein on the insides. Very showy indeed.

GROENKEN'S GLORY   A Dutch variety of compact habit. The blooms are a bright mauve-pink with a unique green eye. One of the most attractive of all.

HARBINGER   Famed for being early, now rare, bearing a large white bloom, but has not so strong a constitution as 'Craddock's White'.

HELGA   A new variety of neat, compact habit, forming a cushion of emerald green, studded with small deep yellow flowers.

ICOME HYBRID   A rare primrose having bloom of a rosy-mauve colour, freely produced.

IRIS MAINWARING   Delicate pure pale blue, flushed pink. The foliage is deep green and the whole is of very compact habit. One of the best primroses and an ideal rockery plant.

JOAN SCHOFIELD   One of the best half-dozen primroses in cultivation. Its huge blooms are wine-red, flushed vermilion, and have a large yellow star-shaped eye. The earliest of all primulas to bloom, flowering for ten weeks.

KINLOUGH BEAUTY   An outstanding primrose, having small dainty flowers of rich salmon-pink with a white candy stripe where the petals overlap. Of sturdy form the blooms are held well above the foliage.

LADY GREER   A superb Irish variety, the dainty polyanthus-type blooms are borne above the foliage. It is a pale yellow counterpart of 'Mrs J. H. Wilson', but has a much longer flowering season. Makes an unusual but charming edging to a herbaceous border.

MISS MASSEY   Old and now almost extinct. Dwarf habit with blooms of a rich bright ruby-red and leaves of bright cucumber green.

MURRAY'S BLUE   It has a stronger constitution than any of the other blues, the purple-blue flowers being marked with red at the centre.

PAM   Dainty crimson-purple, very free flowering over a long period. An ideal rock primula, having the smallest of all blooms.

PAULINE   Rather difficult to rear but well worth the effort. It is very dwarf, having a bloom of intense orange, flushed crimson and yellow.

PERLE VON BOTTROP   Has deep green leaves and bears an early bloom of bright claret-purple held well above the foliage.

PINK FOAM   Of polyanthus form, its pale pink star-like flowers borne on a six-inch stem.

RIVERSLEA   A very dwarf primrose and most uncommon, having dark mauve flowers held well above the cushion-like foliage.

ROMEO   Bears huge vivid parma-violet blooms, flat like a pansy. Very prolific, early, and a strong grower. One of the best primroses in cultivation it is lovely when used as a carpet for yellow tulips.

RUBIN   It has small bronzy-green foliage and comes very early into blooms of bright strawberry-red with a striking yellow eye.

SNOW CUSHION   Of neat habit, it bears small white blooms above bright apple-green foliage.

TAWNY PORT   An attractive, rare little primrose, very dwarf growth and the darkest of all, having maroon-green foliage and dainty dusk port-wine blooms. Of dwarf polyanthus habit, it is from the west of Ireland and is long flowering.

TINY TIM   Like an orange-red 'Pam' and possibly has even smaller bloom. A perfect rockery primula.

VERONICA   A variety of true *Juliae* habit. The flowers are steel-blue with a deep orange centre and are freely produced. A very unusual colour.

WANDA   This variety started the vogue of the *Juliae* primroses. One of the earliest to bloom and latest to finish, the claret-red flowers thrive in full sun and it does well anywhere.

WENDY   Very pale pink, flushed mauve. A large bloom with frilled petals. Easy to propagate and very long flowering.

Hose-in-Hose Primroses

CANARY BIRD   Of semi-polyanthus habit, the vivid yellow blooms are held several to a stem.

ERIN'S GEM   Bears dainty cream blooms.

IRISH MOLLY   The blooms are a delicate shade of rosy-mauve.

IRISH SPARKLER   Most attractive, the small intense scarlet-orange blooms being held in clusters on 9in stems making it grand for cutting.

LADY LETTICE   One of the best of all primroses, the delicate blooms are produced in abundance through spring and are of cream, flushed with apricot and pink, making it a charming plant for a window box or for edging a shrub border or path.

PAM   This is the duplex or hose form of the *Juliae* hybrid and is even more dwarf.

SCOTTISH SPARKLER   Of primrose habit, the blooms are large, almost bell-like and are of true scarlet.

WANDA   The hose form of the ever-popular 'Wanda'.

Jack-in-the-Green Primroses

ELDORADO   A beautiful Jack, the brilliant golden flowers being borne on sturdy polyanthus stems.

MAID MARION   A new Jack, the true primrose yellow blooms having a deeper yellow centre.

ROBIN HOOD   Most attractive in that the carmine-red flowers have a wire edge of white.

SALAMANDER   The bloom, which is of velvety crimson with a striking white spot on each petal, is the largest of all primrose blooms.

TIPPERARY PURPLE   A Jack of the true primrose habit, bearing delicate mauve flowers backed by a ruff of pale green leaves and held on short footstalks.

Polyanthus

'Polyanthus of unnumbered dyes'

JAMES THOMSON

The polyanthus has both *P. veris*, the cowslip, and *P. vulgaris*, the primrose, in its parentage for these species combined to pronounce the hybrid oxlip (as distinct from the true oxlip, *P. elatior*) from which the polyanthus has been evolved. The French botanist Clusius (De l'Ecluse) in his work *Rariorium Plantarum Historia* (1601) described it as *Primula veris pallida flore elatior*, the larger pale-flowered cowslip and like the cowslip, it enjoys a more open situation than *P. elatior*. It was possibly from a crossing of the hybrid oxlip with John Tradescant's Red or Turkie-purple primrose obtained from the Caucasus, that the first red polyanthus or 'big oxlip' was obtained and first described by Rea in his *Complete Florilege* (1665): 'The red cowslip or oxlip is of several sorts, all bearing many flowers on one stalk . . . some bigger, like oxlips' and which must have resembled a polyanthus of inferior quality. It was not until Gertrude Jekyll in 1880 found in her garden a plant bearing yellow flowers, that a polyanthus of this colour was recorded.

The name 'polyanthus' (from the Greek *polyanthos*—'many flowered') so used to describe the plant which, twenty years after the publication of Rea's book had become well known to gardeners, appeared first in *The Florist's Vade Mecum* (1683) by the Rev Samuel Gilbert, who writes: 'There are several oxlips or polyanthuses; I have a very large hose-in-hose of deeper or lighter reds'. Note that always the plants bore red flowers.

Shortly after the publication of Gilbert's work, John Evelyn made reference to the polyanthus, using the word in the modern form, for by then the plant was widely grown for spring display. And, in 1688 appeared the first illustration of a polyanthus, in the *Catalogue* of the Leyden Botanical Garden in Holland, of a plant obtained from the Botanical Garden at Oxford in the year in which the Pilgrim Fathers set sail from Plymouth.

Later, in John Hill's famous work, *The Vegetable Kingdom*, which, having taken sixteen years to write, was published in 1757 and appeared in twenty-five volumes, a coloured illustration shows the polyanthus as being, in the author's own words, 'of a beautiful crimson with an eye of yellow'. In reality, however, the flowers are a purple-crimson, due to fading of the colouring, and with a yellow eye, around which was a striking circle of white which gave the bloom an auricula-like appearance. Careful inspection also reveals a thin wire edging of palest yellow from which we may deduce that the polyanthus had now taken on a new characteristic, on which its fame was to rest for the next hundred years. This was an edging or lacing of the petals of either silver or

The cowslip, *Primula veris*

gold, which was to make the polyanthus as highly esteemed with the florists of the early nineteenth century as the auricula, the laced pink and the ranunculus. A new era in the history of the polyanthus had begun.

Gold-laced Polyanthus

Exactly when the old red-flowered polyanthus took on its golden lacing is lost in obscurity. The red colouring persisted without deviation until about the year 1750 when the blooms took on the striking golden lacing, first revealed in the illustration in John Hill's work. The golden centre may well have been passed on by crossing a red-flowered polyanthus with *Primula pubescens*, a natural hybrid of the crossing of *P. auricula* with *P. hirsuta*, and which is believed to have produced the Alpine auriculas known to Parkinson. Plants of *P. pubescens* are known to have been collected by the botanist Clusius towards the end of the sixteenth century and were grown in the gardens of the Emperor Maximilian II in Vienna. The modern variety 'Kingscote' has flowers of glowing scarlet-cerise with a large, clearly defined golden centre, exactly the same gold as the centre and edging of the laced polyanthus; and similar plants may have been grown in European gardens during the seventeenth century, eventually finding their way to England. The readiness with which almost all members of the primula family hybridise with each other might well have resulted in a hybrid of *P. pubescens* passing on the golden centre to the polyanthus; though this is merely conjecture, there being no record of this having taken place.

By 1760, or perhaps a year or so earlier, the gold-laced polyanthus had become one of the most widely grown of all plants. In 1759, James Justice, who introduced the pineapple to Scotland, wrote from his home at Dalkeith that 'the varieties [of the gold-laced polyanthus] which are obtained every year by the florists who save and sow these seeds, are very great'. It is recorded that in 1769, an exhibition of the plants was held at the home of John Barnes at Lichfield, Staffordshire, this being the earliest reference to the showing of the gold-laced polyanthus.

Year by year the popularity of the laced polyanthus continued to increase and a little publication called *The Polyanthus* which appeared in 1844; listed ninety-six varieties as possessing outstanding qualities. By 1860, several hundred varieties could be obtained and the cult had reached its peak, about a hundred years after the laced polyanthus first appeared. Yet within twenty

Gold-laced polyanthus from an engraving of 1847

years, the greatest of all show winners, Pearson's 'Alexander', had completely vanished. As the mill with its weaving machines took the place of the hand looms in cottages the weavers had to work away from home. No longer were they able to give the necessary care and attention to tending their pots of auriculas and gold-laced polyanthuses.

The old polyanthuses bear blooms which have a golden centre, a red or black ground, and gold lacing round the petals. The body or ground colour is generally black, crimson, red or intermediate shades, and there has never been a laced polyanthus with a ground of any other colour, apart from shades of red in varying degrees of intensity.

Though most of the old florists' favourites have long since disappeared, a few may still be found in cottage gardens. In October 1961, in a letter to the author, a Mr Masters from the south of England told that his family had been growing polyanthuses and primroses in the same garden for more than 160 years, since about the year 1800, and that he had in his collection a polyanthus of maroon-black ground colour and with silver lacing, yet it was previously believed that all traces of the rare silver-laced varieties had vanished years ago.

Even more recently in an Irish cottage garden, the author was shown plants of the old silver-laced double polyanthus, 'Silver Annie', which has flowers of similar mulberry colouring. The lacing is in no way refined but the bloom is semi-double and bears pollen from which it may be possible to raise double polyanthuses in interesting new colours and with the attractive lacing.

In the 1950 *Year Book* of the Northern Section of the National Primula Society, the following passage appeared: 'We are going to have a more difficult job of resuscitation here than with the auriculas, as we have so few parents left . . . I think "Tiny" is the most refined . . .' This variety is one of the few named gold-laced polyanthuses exhibited in the early years of this century and still obtainable.

In America a serious attempt has been made to revive the gold-laced polyanthus chiefly through the enthusiasm of Peter Klein of Tecoma who died before achieving his ambition of raising a strain worthy of comparison with the favourites of old.

Already, interesting results are forthcoming; flowers with almost perfect lacing, conforming in so many ways to the definition of a gold-laced polyanthus as given by the old florists, are now the rule rather than the exception. From this point, amateur growers could take the revival a step further for, unlike the green-edged show auriculas for example, which were the result of mutations (the petals being replaced by leafy structures) and which do not respond to line breeding, the gold-laced polyanthus responds well, while here and there in country cottage gardens, some of the old laced polyanthuses may still survive to form the nucleus of a new collection.

Making an attractive display in a small vase, gold-laced polyanthus

29

Culture

The polyanthus being the result of a cross between the primrose and cowslip may be said to have taken on the characteristics of both plants. It requires an abundance of moisture at its roots during the summer months and whilst it will flourish in shade it is happiest, in the words of Thomas Hogg, 'in a situation exposed to the morning rays of the sun and excluded from them for the rest of the day'. Here again in choice of situation the polyanthus may be said to come halfway between the primrose and cowslip, the former appreciating dappled shade, the latter a position of full sun. The primrose is a flower of the hedgerow, the cowslip of the open meadow especially where low lying, to enable it to receive sufficient moisture. Provided the plants are given an abundance of humus about the roots, the polyanthus will be quite happy in full sun. Where a garden is exposed to the direct rays of the sun, the polyanthus may be grown to the same perfection as where grown in shade, though, as Thomas Hogg has mentioned, shelter from the mid-day sun will prevent the blooms from fading and will ensure an extended flowering season.

A young orchard is the ideal place in which to grow on the plants during summer after they have finished flowering in the beds, when they must be divided and replanted into a humus-laden soil and kept well watered until the new roots have formed.

A light, sandy soil, which tends to dry out in summer, will never grow such sturdy plants as a heavier loam, unless well fortified with humus materials. With a heavy soil, humus is needed to disperse the clay particles so preventing the soil from 'panning' and improving drainage. With a sandy soil humus is required for the retention of as much summer moisture as possible. Where in partial shade, a light soil well enriched with humus should be capable of supporting healthy plant growth even during periods of prolonged dryness. Liberal quantities of peat, used hops, shoddy, old mushroom bed compost and decayed farmyard manure should be incorporated to a depth of at least 18in.

Polyanthuses are best raised from seed sown in boxes or pans in a cold frame. If seed is sown in April, the seedlings will be ready for transplanting to a frame or into the open ground during June. The John Innes sowing compost is suitable. This is composed of 2 parts sterilised loam, 1 part coarse sand, and 1 part peat to which is added per bushel, $1\frac{1}{2}$oz superphosphate of lime and $\frac{1}{2}$oz ground limestone (or chalk). Careful watering at all times after sowing is essential for the seed will not germinate if the compost is dry, whilst the young plants will suffer irreparable harm if allowed to become too dry at the roots. The seed will germinate in about three weeks and the seedlings will be ready to transplant in about a month, spacing them 2 to 3in apart into fresh compost. The plants will come into bloom the following spring.

Early July or springtime is the best time to divide old plants, when the ground is usually damp. The plants should be lifted with care so that the fibrous roots, especially those near the surface, will be in no way damaged. Carefully shake away all surplus soil then, firmly holding the plant, tease apart the various crowns. In this way each crown will have its full quota of fibrous roots, whilst there will be no open wounds as may be the case where the plants are cut into sections. Every crown, however small, will grow into a flowering plant.

Where the plants have formed large clumps which they will do if given good cultivation, they should be divided like any other herbaceous plant, by placing two border forks back to back at the centre of the plant and gently prising apart. The two sections may then be divided as described into numerous offsets and these should be removed to a cool-shaded place without delay and where they remain until ready for replanting as soon as possible. Any unduly large leaves may be screwed off about 3in above the crown before replanting in the same way as when lifting and removing the tops of beetroot, for it is not necessary for the plants to have to re-establish these coarse outer leaves. Offsets with new and smaller leaves should be replanted without the removal of any foliage, for these young leaves will catch the dew and rains and direct the moisture to the roots thus enabling the plants to become more quickly established. The offsets should be set well into the ground and pressed firmly with the hand, or with the foot where the soil is friable. They should be kept well watered until established.

Strains and Varieties

There are a number of polyanthuses which may be the result of a primrose-polyanthus cross, but which because of their long stalk and the formation of a compact flower truss may be classed as of true polyanthus habit. The blooms of each are somewhat daintier than those of the modern polyanthus strains and the plants are of more compact habit. With their intensely rich colouring they are amongst the most attractive of all garden plants. All possess extreme hardiness and are very free flowering.

BARROWBY GEM   With 'Beltany Red' this is one of the finest of all spring plants, ideal for window box or rockery with its sturdy habit. It is now rarely seen, though in the author's garden it grows with the utmost vigour. It is the first polyanthus to come into bloom, the pips opening on a mild February day, whilst the large primrose-yellow shaded with green heads remain colourful until June. It carries a pleasant almond perfume.

BARTIMEUS   This is believed to be a polyanthus of eighteenth century days. It bears a bloom of velvety crimson-black and has no eye. In its place is a region of bronzy red. The blooms are not large nor does it form a large head in comparison with modern standards. It is the Eyeless polyanthus of old garden books, a connoisseur's plant indeed.

BELTANY RED   Origin unknown. It forms a stocky, compact plant and bears a large truss of tangerine-red blooms, which have an unusual green centre and an attractive wire-edge of gold. The leaves are vivid green. The plant remains ten weeks in bloom, and two or three planted together can be seen from afar.

FAIR MAID   The small, but beautifully rounded blooms are freely produced on numerous 15in stems, their colour being burnt orange-scarlet with a most striking double centre of gold. The blooms remain fresh in water for fully two weeks.

HUNTER'S MOON   A modern polyanthus and a beauty, for like 'Barrowby Gem' it comes into bloom before all others and carries a fragrance the equal of the 'Ena Harkness' rose. Of sturdy habit, the bloom is of a lovely shade of apricot with a chrome yellow centre.

RALPH SPOONER   This is possibly the finest double polyanthus ever raised. It bears twenty or more fully double Jersey-cream blooms on each stem, arranged in perfect exhibition form and they retain their perfection over a ong period. Has a soft, sweet perfume.

The double polyanthus, 'Ralph Spooner'

Auriculas

'Auriculas do seem every one of them to be a nosegay alone of itself . . . their pretty scent doth add an increase of pleasure in those that make them ornaments for their wearing.'

JOHN PARKINSON

Since their introduction into England about the year 1575, the border auriculas have come to be cherished in humble and grand garden alike. In the garden of Hardwick Hall in Derbyshire they grow where they may have been since the house was built by Bess, Countess of Shrewsbury. Auriculas are also to be found in the tiny garden of Shakespeare's boyhood home in Stratford-on-Avon.

Not having been confined to pots under glass as have the show auriculas, the older border varieties have in no way lost their vigour and if they can be given a sunny situation and a soil which does not readily dry out during summer, they will prove adaptable to almost every garden, quickly growing into large vigorous clumps above which they bear on 9in stems, irregular heads of large velvety blooms. This irregularity adds to their old-world charm. There is nothing stiff about them and when cut and placed in small vases indoors, they will remain fresh for days and scent the house with their warm sweet honey fragrance. As well as their attractive scent the auriculas have very intense colouring. John Laurance in *The Auricula* has written: 'Nature nowhere discovers her variety of colours, her shades and pretty mixtures, more than in this little flower'.

The Family of Auriculas

The auricula family may be divided into four sections, namely show, alpine, border and the miniatures, named more correctly, *Primula pubescens*. All are extremely hardy though the show auriculas, with their amazing paste-like centres, require protection from the weather, otherwise the meal will 'run' and spoil the bloom if in contact with moisture. They are plants for the specialist grower, demanding great detail in their culture. The true alpine auriculas which are also grown for exhibition should likewise be given the protection of a frame or cold greenhouse for their blooms are of such exquisite colourings that they too are worthy of some protection when coming into bloom. They are, however, completely hardy and may be grown in the open ground together with the old border auriculas. There is always a great demand

An 1833 engraving of the grey-edged show auricula, 'Conqueror of Europe'

for plants of the alpines, which are generally raised and flowered in pots to enable their great beauty to be enjoyed to the full.

The border auriculas may be grown entirely in the open ground, or the offsets may be grown-on in small pots under the same conditions as the alpines and show types. In this case, a cold frame or greenhouse will be required, or a simple structure may be built from timber and Windolite or polythene sheeting, for all that is necessary is to provide pot-grown plants with sufficient light, and to give protection from excessive moisture during winter and from wet weather when plants of the alpines come into bloom during the latter weeks of spring. The plants do not require coddling in any way and stock plants of the alpines should be grown together with the borders, in the open ground, a number being grown-on in pots each year to bloom or to sell. The dainty *pubescens* auriculas or primulas, as they should be more rightly called, are also delightful subjects for growing in small pots indoors or they too may be grown outdoors in the trough garden or about a rockery. There they will appreciate some protection from excess moisture by planting beneath an overhanging stone.

All auriculas are very much like the dianthus family in that they are able to withstand intense cold but are not too tolerant of winter moisture. Where it is not required to exhibit the bloom or grow the plants in pots, then the old border auriculas should be grown, for the beauty of their bloom is exceeded only by that of the alpine and show auricula, the plants being more tolerant of adverse conditions. The auriculas bloom later than the *Juliae* primroses and provide colour during the difficult late spring/early summer period.

Alpine Auriculas

It was Charles Turner of Slough, Bucks., the introducer of Cox's Orange Pippin in 1855, who did so much to improve the alpine auricula a century ago. But for his interest, the lovely 'pures' as they were called, would most certainly have been lost to cultivation.

The alpines may be divided into two groups, those which bear a bloom with a white or light centre, and those having a gold centre. They do not have the paste centre and may be distinguished from the show auriculas in that their foliage is smooth and free from meal. The body colour of the petals shades out to the edges, but that of the self-coloured show varieties is quite uniform.

To bring the alpines to the perfection of which they are capable demands a high degree of skill, but for ordinary purposes their culture can in no way be described as being difficult. It is important where growing all forms of the auricula in pots to use only a small pot, as the plants form only a few fleshy roots which take in moisture and nourishment from the compost extremely slowly. Large pots, full of compost, will quickly become stagnant if there is not sufficient root action to make use of available plant foods, the result being that the leaves will turn yellow and the plants will die back. So use a $2\frac{1}{2}$in pot for the first potting of the offsets which should be detached with a small piece of root. These offsets will form from around the main root stem, two or three appearing each year, and the most suitable time to remove and pot will be soon after the parent plants have flowered in June.

The rich, velvety crimson blooms of the alpine auricula 'Joy'

Compost and Potting

As the plants have to occupy the pots for fully 12 months, they must be quite clean, whilst the compost should be prepared with care. Before adding the compost, small 'crocks' should be placed over the drainage hole. Much has been written about composts for auriculas, from Isaac Emmerton's quite repulsive concoction of 'goose dung steeped in bullock's blood, baker's sugar scum, night soil and yellow loam' to the modern potting composts, but for ordinary purposes the use of a good quality loam will ensure healthy plants without the addition of a large amount of fertiliser. A soil of the right consistency as to proportions of clay and sand, such as Kettering loam, will be ideal or use pasture loam of a fibrous nature and having a 'greasy' feel when rubbed between the fingers.

Peat is not very suitable, for it contains no manurial value, and where using only a small pot it is essential that the maximum amount of food is provided. Old mushroom bed compost, used hops or well-decayed manure, especially cow manure, will be preferable to peat or leaf mould, and they will also keep the compost 'open'. If the loam is of a heavy nature, mix in a little coarse sand and give a dusting of superphosphate to encourage root action. A little powdered charcoal will help to maintain soil sweetness.

The plants will be ready for moving into sixty-size pots by early September, using a similar compost to that used for the first potting. Throughout summer and again after the move to the larger pots, the plants should be allowed to grow on outdoors or in an open frame, the compost being prevented from ever drying-out. Any flower trusses which make their appearance during autumn should be removed, and by early November the plants should be protected from fog and rain. During winter, the plants will require very little moisture, though the compost should not be allowed to dry out. If a hollow sound is to be heard when the pot is tapped, more moisture will be necessary. But during the dormant winter period, do not over-water.

Bringing the Plants into Bloom

Early March and the arrival of warmer weather means that the plants may be given additional moisture to bring them into more vigorous growth. As the sun gathers strength, plants should be shaded by whitening the glass or by fixing brown paper along the sunny side of the structure. The plants will also require the maximum amount of ventilation, for any form of coddling must be avoided. Feeding with diluted manure water once each week will ensure a large bloom and intensify its colourings. Leaves which have become dead and yellow during winter should be removed with care before the flower stems are observed. At the same time the plants may be top-dressed with equal parts loam and decayed manure.

The *pubescens* group will be the first to open their flower-pips under glass, then follow the alpines, and lastly the show varieties, where they are grown. Outdoors, the *pubescens* auriculas, the borders and alpines, will come into bloom in that order, and together with those plants grown under glass will provide brilliant bloom from mid-March until mid-June.

The alpines will form a large flower truss, and where there is overcrowding, the pips or buds should be thinned out so that those remaining may have sufficient room to open fully. Almost complete shading by whitening will prevent the blooms losing colour, whilst every endeavour should be made to maintain as cool conditions as possible so as to prolong the display.

After flowering, the flower-stem should be removed and the plants shaken from their pots, the compost being shaken from the roots. Re-potting should be done without delay using a fresh compost. Any offsets should be removed and potted at the same time. Another circle in the life of an alpine auricula will have begun.

Varieties

Gold Centre

BASUTO The large refined blooms are striking, being of rich crimson-maroon shading to wine-red. The habit of the plant is vigorous.

BOOKHAM BEAUTY A fine new variety, the large well-formed blooms make up a large rounded truss and are of a striking shade of burnt orange shading to pure orange.

BOOKHAM FIREFLY The blooms have a bright, well-defined centre, whilst the glowing crimson colouring shades to maroon. The petals vary from five to seven, whilst the truss is somewhat irregular, but where it does well it is unbeatable.

CICERO An excellent variety for a beginner's collection, for it forms a large truss and is of vigorous habit. The rich maroon blooms with their velvety texture shade out to crimson-red.

CLOTH OF GOLD An outstanding new variety of easy, vigorous habit. The blooms are of rich old gold, shading to pure golden-yellow.

DORIS PARKER It makes a large truss, the medium-sized bloom being of excellent form and of deep crimson-maroon colour shading to bright flame-red.

KINGCUP Crimson, shading to medium brown, it is one of the best gold-centred auriculas ever introduced. The trusses are held well above the foliage, the pips being large and well formed.

NEWTON ABBOT Of vigorous constitution, the blooms, with their large golden centre, are of deepest crimson, shading to red.

PRINCE JOHN One of the best varieties, the centre is larger than most and is of brightest gold, accentuated by the maroon colouring and almost complete lack of shading.

SPARKLE   A magnificent variety, both tube and centre being almost perfect, whilst the body colour is an unusual shade of rich golden-bronze shading to gold.

Light Centre

ARGUS   A fine old variety. It forms an extremely large truss, and though the white centre is not as clearly defined as with some, its rich plum-colour shading to crimson-red is unique and has won for it many premier awards during the past sixty years.

BLUE BONNET   This is a fine blue alpine, but with the continued popularity of 'Gordon Douglas' is not so well known as it deserves to be. The pure white centre is perfectly round and clearly defined, the colour being deep violet-blue shading to mid-blue. Of sturdy constitution, it is easy to grow and propagate.

BOOKHAM GLORY   Carrying the well-known 'Douglas' prefix, it may be relied upon to produce a well-formed truss, the colour being rich royal purple shading to pale heliotrope.

GORDON DOUGLAS   With its creamy-white centre and deep violet-blue flower, this is one of the easiest of all alpine auriculas to manage and propagate, but it must be well shaded when opening its bloom. It is one of the hardiest and most popular of all alpines and a constant winner on the show bench.

JOY   This may be considered to be the premier alpine of its section, being a rich velvety crimson so delicately shaded that it has the appearance of a Show self. It is of vigorous habit and strong constitution.

LADY DARESBURY   One of the finest white-centred alpines ever raised. The very large blooms have eight petals and are of beautiful form with the pips so freely produced that they form a large truss. The colour is rich wine-red, shading to pale cerise, whilst the plant is of strong constitution.

MILLICENT   A striking variety, the deep mauve colouring shading to pale mauve-blue.

MRS HEARN   One of the most beautiful of the alpines with grey-blue, shading to Cambridge-blue flowers. The centre is pale cream, whilst the well-shaped bloom possesses a strong honeysuckle perfume.

PINK LADY   It forms a shapely truss, the blooms being of an attractive wine-pink colour shading to rose-pink.

SPRING MORNING   Of vigorous habit, it forms a well-shaped truss. The bloom are a delicate shade of pink shading to deep rose-red.

Garden Auriculas

Quite distinct from the show and alpine auricula, but equally beautiful and so much easier to grow, the old-fashioned garden auriculas are almost entirely neglected by modern gardeners. They are neglected in more ways than one, for even the few varieties occasionally to be found are generally planted in impoverished soil and have remained unattended for years. Parkinson in his *Paradisus* illustrates seven distinct forms, several being fully double, whilst others were more like cowslips. As many as twenty-one distinct types were described, for the plants were held in esteem as 'a help to pains in the head which may happen by a sight of steep places subject to danger'. The continental painters made great use of their beauty in their flower paintings, in fact few paintings of the seventeenth and eighteenth centuries are to be found without a spray of auriculas. Mountain Cowslips was the name given to plants during later years, denoting their hardiness, and indeed they are amongst the hardiest of all plants, having the dainty *P. hirsuta* and *P. auricula* for parents, these plants being found on the mountainous slopes of Europe from the Alps to the Caucasus.

The garden auriculas will flourish in a soil containing plenty of moisture-holding humus and where they receive some protection from the late spring sunshine. The plants are amongst the easiest of all to grow, being perfectly at home in the cottage garden and also in the smoke-laden atmosphere of the town. Flowering throughout that difficult period of late spring and early summer, the plants are so useful as an edging to a border, or path, or planted to the front of a shrubbery. They may also be planted in beds to themselves. There they may be left to bloom year after year, demanding no more attention than a light mulch each winter and dividing every three years. This is little enough attention to give to so charming a plant and yet few ever take the trouble to provide them with a mulch which may be of decayed manure, leaf mould or peat, and in almost all gardens they are left in dense woody clumps, gradually losing vigour and bearing fewer flowers with each year.

As soon as flowering is over, in early July, the clumps should be divided and the offsets planted into deeply dug soil enriched with a little decayed manure, spent hops, peat or leaf mould. Add some coarse sand or grit and plant in a position where they will receive dappled sunshine, for like the polyanthus they need some sunshine to bring out richness of colouring in the blooms, though exposure to full sunlight will cause the blooms to fade too soon. They must, however, be given a cool, enriched soil, and to correct any sourness of a town soil a little charcoal should be worked in. Division is easily accomplished, and even the smallest offsets should be planted, for they will all flower the following season. The garden auriculas may also be grown in pots in the frame or alpine house when they will bloom throughout the earliest days of spring. Use a 3in pot and a compost as described for the alpine auriculas. Pot-grown plants may be planted at almost any time, though planting during the generally dry months of May and June should be avoided.

To enhance the colour and quality of the bloom occasional waterings with dilute liquid manure will prove rewarding both for plants growing in pots and in the open.

Varieties

Varieties or hybrids of *P. auricula* carry the densely mealed foliage of the parent, hence it is to be found on nearly all the border varieties. The best form of the wild auricula is *P. auricula albo-cincta*, the white-eyed flowers being of a bright golden yellow of the utmost purity and held on tiny 3in stems.

ADAM LORD   An old variety of extremely sturdy habit. The navy-blue flowers with their white centres are held in large trusses above attractively serrated foliage.

BLAIRSIDE YELLOW   This tiny hybrid of *P. auricula* grows only 3in tall and is a charming plant for a trough or sink. It forms rosettes of serrated leaves, similar to those of the *P. pubescens* group, and bears its heads of brilliant yellow over a long period.

BLUE MIST   An outstanding variety, the medium-sized blooms are of purest sky blue, the meal covering providing a silvery sheen.

BLUE VELVET   A very strong grower, the purple-blue flowers with their conspicuous creamy-white centre carry a strong fragrance.

BROADWELL GOLD   Superb, it bears a huge bloom of deep golden-yellow with a white centre. Both bloom and foliage are densely covered with meal.

CELTIC KING   This fine variety bears a bloom of beautiful golden-yellow which possesses a powerful musk-like perfume. The petals are attractively frilled.

CRAIG NORDIE   A lovely and rare variety with its large blooms of burgundy-red and silver-grey foliage.

LINNET   Valuable in that it is very late to bloom and the last to finish. It is well named, for the blooms are a combination of green, brown and mustard, the colourings of the linnet.

MCWATT'S BLUE   The rich mid-blue flowers with their white centre carry a powerful perfume and are held above densely mealed foliage.

MRS NICHOLLS   The pale lemon-yellow blooms have a golden-yellow centre around which is a pure white band or ring.

OLD IRISH BLUE   The bloom, of a beautiful shade of rich, velvety blue with a large white centre, is one of the most richly coloured of all garden plants.

OLD RED DUSTY MILLER   Well named, for the foliage, stem and bloom is heavily mealed, as if covered with flour. The blooms, which are not large, are held on 8–9in stems. The colour is ox-blood red, almost the colour of wallflower 'Belvoir Castle'.

OLD PURPLE DUSTY MILLER   The blooms are lavender-mauve with the silvery

'Buckley's Chloe', a green-edged show auricula

sheen caused by the meal. The stems are longer and less sturdy than those of the other 'Dusty Millers'.

OLD YELLOW DUSTY MILLER   The plants are as heavily mealed as the Red variety, the habit is also the same. The blooms are bright golden yellow, strongly fragrant.

OLD SUFFOLK BRONZE   A delightful variety, bearing a greenish bronze flower which is powerfully scented.

QUEEN ALEXANDRA   Raised in Northern Ireland, this most attractive variety bears a large frilled bloom of pale primrose-yellow and carries a strong fragrance.

ROYAL VELVET   The very large blooms with their attractively frilled petals are of a bright, crimson-purple colour and have a large cream centre.

The Miniature Auriculas *(Primula pubescens)*

This delightful spring flowering plant is very much like the garden auricula. It is indeed the result of a cross between the hardy auricula and the alpine *Primula hirsuta* which carries its heads of bloom on short, sturdy stems, a habit which it has passed on to the *pubescens* group. Here is a plant, perfectly hardy in every way, which should be far more frequently found in our gardens. It produces its richly coloured blooms on 4–5in stems and is a great lime lover. It may be seen at its best on the rockery where it can receive some shade for its roots from nearby stones, whilst at the same time its blooms may enjoy full sunshine.

By planting several varieties the blooms may be enjoyed from mid-April until early June. Apart from the rockery, the plants look delightful when planted by the side of a small path, especially a crazy-paving path, the vivid colour of the blooms showing to perfection against the stones. The *pubescens* primulas are also most valuable plants for a frame or cold greenhouse, planted either in pans or individual pots. Whether growing inside or in the open they enjoy best a compost containing loam and leaf mould in equal parts, to which is added some grit or coarse sand and a small quantity of lime rubble. Provided the plants are kept moist during hot dry weather planting may be done at almost any time, but with this plant the most suitable time for lifting and dividing seems to be as soon as new growth can be seen. This will be early in March. As established plants provide a most glorious display, it is advisable to leave a number each year quite untouched, apart from mulching with some peat over the winter. The rest can be divided and grown-on in small pots. *Primula pubescens* may also be grown from seed which should be sown in pans in a compost similar to that used for potting. May seems to be the most suitable time, fresh seed being used which is merely pressed into the compost, watered and covered with a sheet of glass to hasten germination. Germination may be uneven so remove the seedlings as carefully as possible so as not to disturb those that have yet to germinate.

Varieties

ALBA   Also known as *P. hirsuta alba*, this is a lovely plant unequalled by few for its purity. The large truss is borne on a short, sturdy stem, the blooms carrying a strong perfume.

BLUE WAVE   A glorious variety, the large bright sky-blue flowers have a conspicuous white centre and are extremely fragrant.

COCCINEA   Of compact habit, the large blooms are of a rich brick-red colouring.

COMMODORE   The blooms are of bright crimson-red with a yellow centre and come into bloom before all the other varieties.

FALDONSIDE   Of dwarf habit, it bears its vivid crimson blooms above pale-green rosettes.

FREEDOM   Having the same robust habit of most of the *pubescens* hybrids, it forms a compact plant and bears bloom of bright pansy purple.

GNOME   A delightful little plant, later to bloom than the others. The flowers are bright crimson with a golden centre.

JANET   The large blooms are of a bright blue colour, accentuated by the attractive grey-green leaves.

KINGSCOTE   With 'Gnome', the latest to bloom. The flowers may be described as of glowing cerise, flushed with salmon-orange, accentuated by the large golden eye.

LADYBIRD   The most rare and expensive variety, more difficult to grow than the rest, it being necessary to protect against excess winter moisture. The blooms are rich velvety crimson.

MRS DOUGLAS   A robust and free-flowering variety, bearing bloom of bright petunia-purple with a large white eye.

MRS J. H. WILSON   An old variety, it forms a large truss, the royal purple blooms have a white centre and are strongly fragrant.

RUBY   The well-formed heads are of a lovely shade of wine-pink with a large white eye.

RUFUS   A magnificent vigorous variety, bearing bloom of vivid terracotta scarlet with a brown eye.

THE CARDINAL   A fine old variety, bearing masses of bloom of vivid blood-red. Not to be confused with the double auricula of the same name.

THE GENERAL   Of compact habit, the velvet-red flowers are flushed with orange and produced with freedom.

Pinks

'*Carnation gilliflowers for beauty and delicate smell and excellent properties, deserve letters of gold.*'

STEPHEN BLAKE

Native of the north temperate regions, the pink is able to tolerate extreme cold but it does not enjoy excessive wet. The Athenians held the plant in so great esteem that they named it Di-anthos, Flower of Jove, awarding it the highest honour. It was the chief flower used to make garlands and coronets, hence its early English name of 'coronation' from which the name carnation is a derivative.

It was the opinion of Canon Ellacombe, the Victorian authority on the history of plants, that *Dianthus caryophyllus*, a native of southern Europe, reached England with the Norman invasion, possibly attached to stones imported from northern France by the Conqueror for the erection of castles and churches. It is to be seen to this day, growing on the walls of the castles of Dover and Rochester in Kent, both built by the Normans, and on the walls of Fountains Abbey in Yorkshire where it blooms early in July. Indeed, several of the writers of old believed its country name of 'gillyflower' to be derived from 'Julyflower'.

With the scent of the pinks resembling the perfume of the clove, it was called by the French 'giroflier' which name accompanied the plant to England with the Normans. *D. caryophyllus* takes its botanical name meaning 'nut-leaved' from the name of the clove tree, *Caryophyllus aromaticus*, because the clove scent of the flowers resembled the fragrance of the fruits of that tree. Whether it was *D. caryophyllus* or *D. plumarius* to which Chaucer alluded in the Prologue to *The Canterbury Tales* is uncertain but all those plants bearing clove-scented flowers were at the time much in demand to flavour wine and ale, and pinks, known as sops-in-wine, were to be found until the end of the sixteenth century, growing in tavern gardens everywhere:

> And many a clove gilofre,
> And notemuge to put in ale,
> Whether it be moiste or stale . . .

Chaucer's spelling of the word differs but little from the early French. By Shakespeare's time, it had become 'gillovor' or 'gillyflower', the word being used for all clove-scented flowers, such as the Queen's Gillyflower (*Hesperis matronalis*) and the Stock Gillyflower.

By Tudor times, there would appear to be two groups of dianthus, those with single flowers, known as the pinks and descended from *D. plumarius* and those bearing double (or semi-double) flowers, offspring of *D. caryophyllus*. In the *New Herbal* of 1578, Lyte distinguished between the two forms by his use of the word 'coronations' and of 'the small feathered gillofers, known as Pynkes, Soppes-in-Wine and small Honesties'.

The earliest carnations (or semi-double pinks) bore flowers of flesh colour which may be described as deep 'pink' and alluded to in Shakespeare's *Henry V* when, in Mistress Quickly's house in Eastcheap, the Boy says '. . . and [he] said they were devils incarnate'. To which Mistress Quickly replies: 'A could never abide carnation; 'twas a colour he [the dead Falstaff] never liked'. That there were at the time, 'streaked gillyflowers' is confirmed both by Shakespeare and in the *Book of Flowers* by Maria Merian, a copy of which is in the British Museum, London, and in which there is a colour illustration which shows the 'streaked gillyflowers' much as we know the flaked carnations of today.

At the time of Shakespeare's death, carnations and pinks had become amongst the most popular of all garden plants. Gerard wrote that '. . . they are well known to most, if not to all' and William Lawson in *The Country Housewife's Garden* (1618) said, 'I may well call them the king of flowers, except the rose'.

Varying in colour from deep pink to almost white, and strongly clove-scented, these pinks have grown for centuries among the ruined masonry of Fountains Abbey in Yorkshire

Their popularity was possibly due to their hardiness and, though native of south and eastern Europe, they quickly became acclimatised to English gardens, being most suitable for the small 'knotted' beds of the time.

The Laced Pink

The early nineteenth century was perhaps the Golden Age of the pink, and in *The Flower Garden* (1839) M'Intosh has listed 192 varieties, including several which were introduced by such well-known florists of that time including Barlow, Hogg and Keen. M'Intosh mentions that 'it is pre-eminently the cottager's flower as it takes less care and skill to cultivate than the carnation and other florist's flowers'. Thomas Hogg, a nurseryman of Paddington Green, writing in 1822, lists 121 varieties in his *Catalogue of Pinks*, and in addition, a dozen Scottish pinks, one of which had the charming name of 'Robertson's Gentle Shepherd'. That there must have been many varieties of the pink during Hogg's time is obvious in reading the introduction to his *Catalogue* for he says, '. . . and if I have not published a numerous list, let it be remembered that quality, in respect of flowers, is always preferable to quantity'. And he then lists his 121 varieties!

In the same way that the miners of Yorkshire and Derbyshire took up the culture of the pansy, and the cotton workers of Lancashire devoted their hours of leisure to the show auricula, so did the Scottish weavers of Paisley toil to reproduce the intricate oriental patterns of their shawls on the flowers of the pink. Their object was to impart the characteristic of rounded or smooth edges to the flowers, thereby eliminating the serrated petal edges of *D. plumarius*. At the outer edge of the petals was to be a band of black or red or purple, with which colouring the blooms were also marked at the centre. The variety was recognised by the degree of black, red or purple about the bloom.

Each group of florists had their own particular favourites which they exhibited at the pink shows up and down the country, possibly the most highly valued variety being 'Lustre', a purple, laced pink which took the premier awards throughout the 1830s. Requiring a clean atmosphere, the Paisley pinks flourished until the factory took over from the hand loom, until the tall chimneys began to belch out their blackened smoke and dirt which was soon to cover the countryside and which has continued ever since.

Culture

The florists of old, almost without exception, made mention of the pink's liking for a well-drained soil and an open, sunny situation but surprisingly they made no mention of the plant requiring a soil containing plenty of lime. Large quantities of manure as for auriculas was the order of the day and this more than anything may have contributed to the rapid decline of the florists' pinks. A top dressing of manure made for a 'soft', disease-prone plant and few varieties survived for long.

Primroses: 1 Double white (*alba plena*); 2 *lilacina plena*; 3 Marie Crousse;
4 Bon Accord Purple

Pinks: 1 Sweetheart Abbey; 2 Dad's Favourite; 3 Dusky; 4 London Glow;
5 Solomon

Thomas Hogg wrote that 'florists contending for a prize and anxious to get the plants large, would leave three blooms only on each stem, and four or five stems to a plant . . . As soon as the pods are well formed, they tie a piece of raffia around them, to prevent their bursting irregularly and as soon as in bloom, place a glass and other covering over them to protect them from rain and sun, thus preserving their colours from being faded and tarnished'.

Hogg has told that a pink bed will continue to flower well for two years in succession (it will do so indefinitely if top dressed with lime), though most florists renew their plants yearly by 'piping the grass'. This is the old florists' term for propagation by pipings which are the non-flowered shoots. They are removed with two pairs of leaves by pulling them in an upwards direction.

Hogg began to take his pipings on 21 June and Joseph Paxton, when head gardener at Chatsworth House, the Duke of Devonshire's seat, said that his pipings were taken 'about the middle or end of June, never later than the first week of July when they should be about 2in long'. Paxton recommended that they be inserted in beds of sandy soil, planting them about 3in apart. Pipings may also be planted in a frame or in boxes, in a sandy compost, keeping them moist and shaded from the sun when they will root in about four weeks.

Pinks may also be propagated from slips. These are cuttings removed from the main stems at the base of the plant. They are taken with a 'heel' and will readily root in a sandy compost. Pinks are also propagated by removing the shoots at a node, either by cutting them or breaking them off. Carnations are increased by layering (see Chapter 6).

The beds are made up in early autumn, planting 9in apart because pinks spread rapidly and form large clumps. They require an open, sunny situation and a well-drained soil containing plenty of lime rubble which is also given each year as a top dressing. Pinks can endure long periods without moisture and do better in the eastern part of the UK than in the west. Only when the buds are forming and until the flowers have opened, do the plants need care with their watering.

To prevent those large flowering varieties from bursting their calyces, the florists assisted nature by 'letting down the pod', which is done with a penknife, to make slits around the calyx so that all parts of the flower will open at the same time and so preserve the symmetry of the bloom. Another innovation was to place a circular card beneath the calyx so that when it opened, the outer or guard petals would rest against it, covering it entirely, thus giving the flower a symmetrical appearance.

Fourteenth Century Pinks

FENBOW'S NUTMEG CLOVE   It is one of the oldest garden plants still in cultivation, dating from the fourteenth century. It was rediscovered in 1960, in the north of England growing in the garden of Colonel Fenbow in whose family are

preserved records to say that the Nutmeg Clove was growing in the same garden in 1652, planted there by a certain Julian Fenbow to impart its powerful nutmeg scent to flavour wines. It bears a small but fully double flower of crimson-maroon with slightly feathered petals and measures little more than 1in across. The leaves are blue-green and upright.

SOPS-IN-WINE   A plant of this name still survives and may be the original of Chaucer's time for it is believed to have reached England during the early years of the fourteenth century, from a European monastery garden which is believed to be situated near Orleans. It flourishes in cottage gardens in Berkshire where it is still called by its ancient name. The white flower is extremely fringed and has a black central zone whilst its perfume resembles that of the 'Old Nutmeg Clove' carnation.

Fifteenth Century Pinks

CAESAR'S MANTLE   The 'Bloody Pink' of early Tudor and Elizabethan times, it may well date from the end of the fifteenth century. It bears a flower over an inch in diameter, of a dark blood-red colour, covered in a grape-like 'bloom'. The crimson-red becomes almost black at the centre whilst the petals are deeply toothed. Has a powerful clove scent.

Sixteenth Century Pinks

FOUNTAINS ABBEY   Resembling the equally old 'Queen of Sheba' in appearance, the flowers being less than 1in in diameter but semi-double. The petals are beautifully fringed whilst the black lacing on a white ground is the equal of the old Scottish pinks.

NONSUCH   Of 'Painted Lady' type and is believed to have been discovered in the gardens of Henry VIII's palace of Nonsuch though it may have received its name from its great beauty. The petals are more deeply fringed than others of this type whilst the ground colour is pink with ruby-red flashes.

OLD MAN'S HEAD   Dating from the early seventeenth or late sixteenth century and rediscovered in a N. Yorkshire garden. It is a sturdy grower bearing white semi-double flowers, curiously spotted and splashed with purple and with a powerful clove perfume.

PAINTED LADY   It was rediscovered in 1950, growing in a Welsh garden and resembles in all characteristics an illustration of 'Ye Gallan't Fayre Ladye'

Laced pinks from *The Florist*, 1848: (*left*) 'Mr Edwards' and (*right*) 'Young's Double X'

pink which appears in a book of garden flowers of the first year of James I's reign. It bears a bloom only 1in across and is semi-double with fringed petals which are white, flashed with purple.

QUEEN OF SHEBA   A pink of the 'Painted Lady' type, bearing single flowers 1in across, with neat serrated petals which are laced with magenta-purple on a white ground. Of the late Elizabethan era, either late sixteenth or early seventeenth century.

UNIQUE   Of the same age as those surviving members of the 'Painted Lady' type. The flowers are single and of outstanding beauty, the ground colour being red and covered all over with flashes of black and pink.

Seventeenth Century Pinks

BAT'S DOUBLE RED   Has been growing in the Botanical Gardens at Oxford since the end of the seventeenth century and is believed to be that raised by a Thomas Bat in London and was until 1950, believed to be lost. It has blue-green foliage and bears flowers with bluntly toothed petals of rich ruby red, over a long period.

BRIDAL VEIL   One of the old fringed pinks, possibly of the late seventeenth century, the double blooms of ice white, having a crimson patch at the base of each petal. They are heavily scented.

FIMBRIATA   Its origin is lost in antiquity but it is most likely a late Elizabethan pink, the creamy-white flowers with their fringed petals having pronounced perfume.

GREEN EYE   Also 'Charles Musgrave' or 'Musgrave's Pink', named after the owner of the cottage garden where it was rediscovered. It is said to be identical with plants which have been growing in the Palace garden at Wells since the end of the seventeenth century. The blooms are single, of 1½in diameter and are of purest white, with slightly fringed petals which overlap and they have a conspicuous green eye or zone. They have outstanding fragrance.

OLD FRINGED   One of the oldest pinks in cultivation, most likely grown in gardens of the late Elizabethan period. Of dwarf, compact habit, and bearing semi-double flowers of purest white with extremely fringed petals and of exquisite clove perfume. It was used by Montagu Allwood as the seed-bearing parent of the first *allwoodii* pink.

PHEASANT EYE   One of several pinks surviving from the early seventeenth century though each of them may be older. It is to be found in both the single and semi-double form with the petals deeply fringed whilst the ground colour is white or blush, with a conspicuous purple-brown 'eye' at the centre. Occasionally the flowers have lacing of the same colour.

Eighteenth Century Pinks

BEVERLEY PINK   It was found in a cottage garden of a Mr Williams at Beverley in N. England where it had grown since at least early in the century.

Now rare, the unusual old English pink, 'Queen of Sheba', survives from the
seventeenth century

The small semi-double blooms of crimson-red are flaked with white and yellow and have the true clove perfume.

CHELSEA PINK   Also 'Little Old Lady'. It was to be found in Chelsea gardens early in the century. It is like a 'Painted Lady', with glorious perfume, the small double flowers of crimson-red being edged and splashed with white.

GLORIOSA   An old Scottish pink, possibly having a carnation for one parent for the flowers are of beautiful shape and fully double, being of pale pink colouring with a crimson eye and having outstanding fragrance.

INCHMERY   Makes a neat compact plant and bears a profusion of double flowers which open flat without splitting their calyces and are of an attractive shade of bright clear pink acting as a pleasing foil for the silvery foliage. It has outstanding perfume.

MONTROSE PINK   Also known as the 'Cockenzie Pink' as it was discovered in the Scottish fishing village of that name, found growing in the garden of Montrose House where it has been since early in the century. It is still listed by Forbes of Hawick and is a beauty, growing 9in tall and bearing on stiff stems, fully double blooms of brilliant carmine-pink.

Nineteenth Century Pinks

AVOCA PURPLE   May be very much older for it is to be found in many Co. Wicklow cottage gardens. It bears a small purple flower, streaked with lines of darker purple and it is sweetly scented.

BLACK PRINCE   An old Irish variety now rarely seen and somewhat resembling 'Sops-in-Wine', its semi-double flowers being white with a large black centre or eye and with similar nutmeg scent.

EARL OF ESSEX   One of these much loved garden pinks which usually splits its calyx but is always welcomed in the garden. The clear rose-pink blooms with their fringed petals have a small dark zone and sweet perfume.

EMILLE PARÉ   One of the truly outstanding pinks, raised in 1840 in Orleans, France, by André Paré, probably having the Sweet William for one parent for it bears its double salmon-pink flowers in clusters and will survive only a few years so that it should be propagated annually.

LINCOLNSHIRE LASS   It has been known since the beginning of the century and may be much older. The flowers are of an uninteresting flesh colour but its scent makes it worthy of cultivation.

MRS SINKINS   Raised by a Mr Sinkins, Master of Slough Workhouse, and named after his wife, the plant has the distinction of being incorporated in the Arms of the Borough of Slough. It is a pink of great character, its large white cabbage-like blooms borne on 12in stems above a mat of silvery-green foliage, possessing an almost overpowering perfume.

PADDINGTON   This was raised about 1820 by Thomas Hogg, a nurseryman of that part of London on which now stands Paddington Station. Of dwarf habit, its double pink blooms have serrated edges and are richly scented.

ROSE DE MAI   It may be traced back to the beginning of the century. The double blooms are creamy-mauve with fringed petals and glorious perfume.

RUTH FISCHER   Dating from the end of the century, it is a most attractive variety of compact habit and bears small fully double flowers of purest white with a rich, sweet perfume.

SAM BARLOW   At one time it was to be found in every cottage garden though is now rarely seen. Like 'Mrs Sinkins' and so many of the old double pinks it splits its calyx but blooms in profusion, its white flowers having a maroon blotch at the centre and with a penetrating clove perfume.

WHITE LADIES   Bears sweetly scented blooms of purest white throughout the summer which do not split their calyces. Obviously a variety of D. plumarius, for it has the same fringed petals, it is a plant of neat habit and is tolerant of all conditions.

Twentieth Century Pinks

DUSKY   The results of back crossing the 'Old Fringed' pink with an *allwoodii* seedling and it is free and perpetual flowering. The blooms have fringed petals and are dusky-pink.

ENID ANDERSON   A striking pink, its semi-double clove-scented flowers of glowing crimson being enhanced by the silver-grey leaves.

GUSFORD   An outstanding scented pink, bearing large double blooms of rosy-pink on 12in stems.

HASLEMERE   The large fragrant double flowers have a deep chocolate centre and fringed petals.

ICE QUEEN   A 'sport' from 'Dusky', it bears a highly scented double bloom of icy white which does not burst its calyx and which has fringed petals.

LILAC TIME   An Imperial pink bearing fully double blooms of lilac-pink with a powerful scent.

Laced Pinks Varieties

These laced pinks are still obtainable, though are rare:

CHARITY   The habit is short and tufted whilst the plant is free flowering. The semi-double blooms have a white ground with clearly defined lacing of bright crimson.

DAD'S FAVOURITE   Also known as 'A. J. Macself'. The blooms which are semi-double open flat and circular, the pure white ground being laced with ruby-red.

FAITH   The first of the laced *allwoodii* (1946). The blooms are small but fully double with the petals broad and fringed. The ground colour is rosy-mauve with lacing of cardinal-red.

58

JOHN BALL. Raised and introduced by Turner of Slough about 1880. The bloom is large and double with a white ground and has lacing and zoning of velvet-purple.

LONDON SUPERB The large double blooms have a pale pink ground and are laced with purple. The fringed petals and perfume give it the old-world charm.

MURRAY'S LACED A delightful pink, it was rediscovered in 1949 and whilst the semi-double blooms are small, the ground is pure white and the lacing clean, of a beautiful shade of mulberry-red. This may also be one of the old Paisley pinks.

SMITH'S SUPERB BLUSH It was illustrated in *The Floricultural Magazine* for 1 June, 1835, and is believed to be named after E. D. Smith, the artist of Sweet's *Florist Guide*. The bloom was large and of deep rose-pink with heavy lacing of deep crimson. It was to be obtained until recent times though may now be extinct.

VICTORIAN A laced pink of early Victorian times bearing huge blooms which often burst their calyx but is a most attractive variety. The white ground is zoned and laced with chocolate.

WILLIAM BROWNHILL It dates from about 1780 and is one of the best of the laced pinks, the beautifully formed blooms being white, laced and zoned with maroon and they do not burst their calyces. Still obtainable.

'Murray's' laced pink

Border Carnations

'Let yon admired carnation own,
Not all was meant for raiment, or for food
Not all for needful use alone;
There, while the seeds of future blossoms dwell,
'Tis colour'd for the sight, perfumed to please the smell.'

SHENSTONE

Plants of extreme hardiness and of easy culture, the border carnation has for long been a collector's plant. Being evergreen, with attractive silvery green foliage, the borders could well be more widely planted, not only for bloom for the show bench, but as an edging to a path or along a terrace. They also make excellent bedding plants, being particularly attractive in a raised circular bed. Even when the plants have finished blooming the beds will remain tidy and fully evergreen. So exquisite are the colourings of the border carnations that of all garden flowers they may be classed as being true florists' flowers in the same way as were the gold-laced polyanthus and the auricula of a previous century. For years they have been cultivated by the enthusiastic gardeners of the industrial North and Midlands. There they are to be found growing in prepared beds in allotment gardens, to be tended with loving care during summer evenings and at weekends. There are growers who have specialised in these plants for fifty years or more, growing but one or two plants of each variety. Through the years, collections have been built up numbering a hundred or more varieties, cuttings and plants being exchanged or sold in the local public-house where enthusiasts meet at the end of the day, always ready to obtain something new to add to their collections. To cater for these enthusiasts, specialist growers, often beginning in the same way, in an allotment or back garden with not more than a dozen varieties, devote acres of ground to the culture of the border and garden pinks, which are able to tolerate deposits of soot and sulphur formed where growing in the industrial areas, and which are completely hardy and labour saving.

Soil Requirements

All members of the *Dianthus* family require an open, sunny position, and the borders are no exception. Not even in partial shade will they be happy and where they cannot be given full sun they should not be grown. Hence they are so often better where grown in an allotment, generally a part of an open field, than in a back garden where only limited sunshine may penetrate. Border carnations are able to withstand intense cold, indeed they grow best under such conditions, always enjoying the cold, dry climate of the north-east very much better than the humid warmth of the south-west. With their liking for full sunshine goes a tolerance for dry soil conditions and no plant will give a better account of itself in a shallow, dry soil than the border carnation. Such a soil is to be found where it contains a large proportion of lime or chalk. On such land the border is at its best, for the plants will never prove successful where their diet is lacking in lime.

Border carnations do not require an abundance of manure and humus in the soil in the same way as do members of the primrose family, but they must have lime and a well-drained soil. For this reason they are best grown in a raised bed to which shingle has been added where the soil is of a heavy nature. Borders will grow well in a heavy soil which is well drained, and some of the finest plants I ever grew were planted in clay soil on a northerly slope which allowed winter moisture to drain away readily. Should the soil contain a large proportion of clay particles, give a dressing in early winter of caustic (unhydrated) lime. This will heat up upon contact with moisture in the soil and a violent reaction will occur. At the same time the clay particles of the soil will disintegrate. The plants will, in addition, benefit from the lime. Where the soil is friable loam of medium texture, then neither manure nor drainage materials will be necessary. Give a liberal dressing of hydrated lime a month before planting, and especially is this necessary for a town garden where the soil is often of a high acid content. Also work in some wood ash, for the potash content will enhance the colour of the bloom.

The ground should be brought to a fine tilth before planting whilst all perennial weeds should have been eradicated. This is absolutely essential, for the best method of propagating borders is by layering and it is difficult to layer in weed-infested ground. Also, once established, borders resent disturbance for their roots are nothing like as fibrous as those of many other hardy plants and to remove deeply rooting weeds may cause the carnations to die back. Border carnations are always happy where following a crop of potatoes which will clean the soil and bring it to the necessary fine tilth. The residual manure will also benefit the plants and all that is needed before planting will be to give a dressing with lime or to work in a quantity of lime rubble. The plants will also benefit from a 2oz per sq yd dressing with sulphate of potash at planting time.

Planting

Without hesitation I would always recommend planting border carnations early in spring, as soon as the ground is friable after the winter weather. The plants will then grow away rapidly and will not remain dormant for several months as they will when planted in the autumn. This may not be detrimental where the ground is very well drained, but if an excess of moisture remains about the roots they will not be sufficiently active during winter to absorb this moisture and will most assuredly decay. In addition, to allow the soil to become weathered during winter will ensure a fine tilth. So plant during March and April, using pot-grown plants so that the roots will be disturbed as little as possible.

The ideal plant for setting into the open ground in spring is one from either a 2½in or 3in pot; a sturdy bushy plant which has been grown from a layer rooted the previous July and potted in September to winter in a cold frame until March. This will have become a hardy, vigorous plant capable of producing a number of choice blooms the first summer.

Before ordering the plants it is always a sound policy to see them growing in the pots so that one knows just what type of plants to expect. When buying from one of the world-renowned commercial houses this may not be necessary, but any good firm will appreciate a visit from a customer. Visit the shows and see the many wonderful varieties in the 'flesh', for catalogue descriptions are often deceptive. In any case, do not expect to be able to grow bloom equal to that seen at the shows until many years have been spent amongst carnations. Remember, too, that the bloom at the show has been selected from hundreds and maybe even thousands of choice flowers. Another point to take into consideration is the variation in the colour of many varieties grown on different soils. I have known several lovely deep orange shades show themselves in a very washed-out form in other gardens.

When ordering your selection, take particular care to ask the supplier to send by passenger train in boxes which are left open at the top so that there will be no breakage through careless handling. The plants will be knocked out of the pots and a sheet of paper fastened round the ball of soil sent with each plant. This is a point for all carnation growers to observe, for the correct presentation of the stock is equally as important as the quality of the plants. Plants of this nature vary in price, depending upon whether they are old or new introductions. The cheaper plants may be equally as good as those generally priced higher. They will most probably be cheap because of their freedom to produce a large number of shoots suitable for layering, or they may be old favourites of which most nurserymen have built up a large stock. The number to purchase at first will, of course, be decided by capital and area of land available. I should begin with at least a dozen different varieties but possibly twenty will give a wider choice as there are so many to choose from, all of which produce a brilliant show. The amateur enthusiast will add just one or two new varieties each year; the commercial grower will add possibly a hundred plants of several new introductions. A good crimson, a salmon-pink, a white, yellow-mauve and orange self must be in every collection; two yellow ground and two white ground varieties and finally two fancies would make an excellent beginning.

As soon as the plants arrive, they should be removed from their boxes and stood on the floor of a cool room and lightly watered. There they may remain for a day or two until the ground receives a final raking, or harrowing, if the planting is to be on a large scale. When the ground is in just the right condition the plants should be set out very firmly, but should not be put in too deeply for this will cause rotting of the stem. The plants should be placed about 2ft apart each way to allow room for layering and room for weeding. During a dry spell of weather, each plant should be watered individually and this will be sufficient for them to become fully established. Carnations love the sun, as much as they can possibly obtain, though as far as wind is concerned they will put up with much inconvenience. Not being tall-growing, they require little or no staking, and so only the minimum of protection need be provided. They are able to stand up to dry conditions very much better than will, say, scabious, sweet peas and chrysanthemums. For this reason the dianthus family probably requires less attention than any other of our choice border flowers.

When growing in beds for garden decoration, planting should be 15in apart, so as to give a massed effect, for borders are at their loveliest when seen in this way. Only one colour or variety should be planted in each bed. Never forget to name all varieties with wooden labels.

Staking and Disbudding

During the summer months, the plants will require little attention except for keeping the ground free from all weeds. Regular hoeing is a wonderful help towards the building up of a strong plant. By the end of April new growth will be observed, and by the beginning of May the flowering shoots will have made great headway. Almost daily the stems seem to lengthen and the buds become more swollen. Now comes the first attention to be given to the border and that is the removing of all unwanted buds which appear clustered round the centre or main bed. This may be done either with the fingers or by using a blunt knife. I prefer my fingers and it is surprising how quickly a hundred or more stems may be disbudded when once one has become accustomed to the work. Should the main bud be removed by mistake, then allow one of the smaller buds to remain, for this will produce a flower almost as good in every way. At the same time as the bud is taken, the stem should be made secure to a 2ft bamboo cane by means of a wire ring placed over the top and allowed to rest on a leaf joint. Wire rings cost only a few pence per hundred and not only may they be used over and over again but they are so much quicker than raffia or string, both of which may cut through the stem during windy weather.

When removing the surplus buds around the main bud care must be taken not to confuse this operation with thinning the side shoots growing from the main stem. Each of these will produce excellent blooms ideal for cutting or for garden decoration, and should be disbudded in the same way as for the main stem bud. If the blooms are required for exhibition purposes, then the weaker shoots should be removed to allow the other to reach maturity by drawing on the food reserves of the plant. Throughout the summer stems will be branching from almost every leaf-joint and from the base of the main stem though possibly half must be removed as surplus. This freedom of producing stems greatly extends the flowering season. Should it be the aim of the grower to be producing as much colour in his garden as possible, then little or no serious disbudding will be necessary.

Propagation

The commercial grower of borders who does not grow for cut bloom but only to obtain as many layers for sale as possible, removes most of the flower stems when young so as to conserve the vitality of the plant, for it is too much to ask a young plant to produce both a quantity of cut bloom, and a large number of layers each season, year after year. Few or no layers are taken until the second season.

The bloom should be cut during the early morning, if possible before the dew has left the petals, and the stems should be placed in buckets of cold water for an hour before packing. The market salesman favours single colours to each box, and for this reason, the cut flower grower should plant a sufficient number of plants of each variety to produce a worth-while quantity of bloom at each cutting, for flower-boxes will hold at least two dozen bunches. If a small label is placed with each bunch, together with the grower's name or trade mark, this will do much to encourage buying of young plants each season.

Layering in the Open

Though borders may be grown from cuttings and by sowing seed, plants from the former tend to weaken in constitution, whilst those from seed cannot be relied upon to come true to colour and form. Layering, then, is the only really certain method of propagation and is frequently the most practical. The treatment of cuttings is almost exactly as described in Chapter 4 on pinks and will not be enlarged upon here.

Layering is done in July in the north, but the period may with safety be extended until the third week in August in the south where the rooting periods last until early October. Too early layering should be avoided as the plants may become lanky during a wet, late summer when they will make too much growth before the autumn frosts arrive to cause them damage. Layering frequently seems to cause the border enthusiast considerable worry, but why I do not know. To anyone with a careful hand, and most gardeners possess this quality, layering is as easy as taking cuttings and infinitely more sure in rooting.

Almost all plants will produce a number of shoots which are close enough to the soil for layering and, by taking a sharp knife and cutting carefully up to the joint which is nearest to the soil, very many may be layered in a day. The

Carnations from a coloured engraving of 1850

cut should be made up the centre of the stem about an inch in length and should not be taken beyond the joint. Care must be taken not to sever the cutting from the parent plant. The portion of stem which is not connected to the plant is then bent upwards and firmly pressed into the soil. A wire pin bent in the form of a hairpin is placed round that portivin connecting cutting to parent and pressed into the soil to prevent the cutting from leaving the ground.

Continuing to obtain its nutriment from its parent, the layer will quickly take root, how soon depending upon the degree of moisture in the soil. The time taken is about four weeks under normal conditions compared with twice as long for cuttings severed from the parent. The layer will suffer little either from too wet or too dry conditions though, of course, quickness in rooting depends upon a certain amount of help from the grower. Before any attempt at layering is made, the soil must be quite clear of all weeds and should have had a top dressing of peat and coarse sand in which it is to root. Careful hoeing round each plant before adding the top dressing will do much to retain the moisture content of the soil.

Many amateurs place cloches or sheets of glass over their layers. This may be a help during a cold wet period but is not really necessary for first-class rooting results. During the rooting period little disturbance should be necessary, apart from removing an occasional weed and giving a watering should the soil become hard and dry, and this is frequently the case during the generally hot month of August. By the middle of the month one or two layers should be carefully lifted to find how the rooting system is progressing and, if satisfactory, each should be cut from the parent plant and allowed to remain in position for a few days before potting into $2\frac{1}{2}$in pots. This does not cause too great a shock to the young plant.

Layering in Pots

Some gardeners prefer to layer the shoots directly into these small pots which are inserted into the ground and allowed to protrude about half an inch above the soil level. The reason for this method is twofold. First, they contend that the layers root more quickly if pegged down by the side of the pot and secondly, that the young plants receive no check when severed from the parent plant. Against these points it must be said that all plants in pots require much more careful watering than plants in the open ground, and unless this extra attention can be given, layering should take place in the normal way. Whichever method is utilised, care must be taken to keep the layer in an upright condition otherwise the plant will become bent.

When the rooted layers have been severed from the parent they are potted into small pots containing a mixture of well-rooted turf loam, peat and a little sand. They are then moved to cold frames which are allowed to remain open during a mild winter, or they may be moved to a sheltered place where they

Border Carnations

Violas: 1 Irish Molly; 2 Androsse Gem; 3 Bluestone; 4 Jackanapes;
5 Chantryland; 6 Dobbie's Bronze

are allowed to remain in the open on beds of rubble and ashes. Care must be taken to name each batch of plants very clearly, for there is nothing more annoying than to receive what subsequently turns out to be a mauve bloom when a vivid scarlet has been ordered. It does not enhance the reputation of the nurseryman. Careful watering will be necessary after once the young plants have been watered in their new pots, and by late March they will be making bushy plants highly suitable for border carnation enthusiasts.

Care of the Plants

It cannot be said that as soon as the plants reach the pots they may be left to take care of themselves. Watering will be a source of constant worry, and attacks from slugs a never-ending menace. It may happen that a very warm spell of weather is experienced during late autumn. I know that in the north in recent years warmest days of the year have been in September and October, which cause the soil in the pots to dry out quickly if the plants are not afforded some shade during daytime. Danger time is the night, when a severe ground frost follows hot sunshine and a pot wet with water. Shading is better than giving too much water; as little water as possible should be the motto. By November all the moisture needed by the plants will be obtained from the atmosphere and it should be quite unnecessary to give artificial moisture.

Attacks from slugs are often a source of trouble during a wet autumn and winter. Preparations for killing these pests should be sprinkled between the rows of pots; common salt is an excellent deterrent.

If the plants are kept in closed frames during the winter, they should be given as much fresh air as possible as soon as any severe weather has departed. Rarely, if ever, should the frames be closed completely for borders just will not tolerate a stuffy atmosphere. Late February will see more 'open' conditions, which is the sign for the lights to be completely removed by degrees and a little more water to be given.

When the plants are ready for planting out they should be carefully knocked from the pots, having been watered the day previously to help to bind the roots.

Varieties

Crimson and Scarlet Selfs

BONFIRE   The blooms, of beautiful form, are of a vivid cardinal-red colour, held on strong erect stems.

BOOKHAM GRAND   It is a plant of extreme vigour, the huge blooms being of rich wine-red which are of perfect form.

DAMASK CLOVE   Deep crimson blooms with petals like velvet and a powerful clove perfume.

FIERY CROSS   A fine scarlet self of perfect shape. A true exhibition variety, having all the good points.

GIPSY CLOVE   One of the finest of all borders with a vigorous habit and bearing a massive bloom of glowing crimson.

OAKFIELD CLOVE   A huge flower of excellent formation and having the true clove scent. The colour is a bright crimson and the foliage a vivid green with no trace of blue.

PERFECT CLOVE   The glowing scarlet-crimson blooms are borne with great freedom.

W. B. CRANFIELD   A magnificent scarlet self of vigorous habit. Bloom is very free, stem and calyx strong. Excellent both for exhibiting and for cutting, it has never been surpassed in its colour.

Apricot and Orange Selfs

BRENDA BARKER   A pure apricot self of vigorous, free-flowering habit.

DALESMAN   Large perfectly formed blooms of a rich apricot-orange shade.

ESMOND LOWE   The border counterpart of the market grower's perpetual carnation, 'Tangerine'. The bloom is small, but of a lovely golden-orange colour and its freedom of flowering is remarkable.

KING LEAR   In the author's opinion, one of the most perfect borders ever introduced. The huge blooms are of a rich tangerine colour and freely produced on strong stems.

LOYALIST   One of the finest of all borders, being extremely free-flowering and bearing a neat, medium-sized bloom of brilliant nasturtium orange.

OPHELIA   The blooms are large, of exhibition form and are deep apricot.

Pink Selfs

BOOKHAM PEACH   Of perfect exhibition form, the huge blooms are malmaison pink.

DAWN CLOVE   It is a strong grower and bears with freedom its perfect blooms of porcelain-pink.

HUNTER'S CLOVE   The colour may be best described as being of hunting pink or glowing rose-pink and of perfect form.

LUCY ASHTON   Possesses all the good points of 'Queen Clove' and bears a large bloom of camellia-pink.

QUEEN CLOVE   One of the best of all borders, of strong vigorous habit with a rigid stem and perfect calyx. The colour is begonia-rose.

QUEEN MAB   An older variety, but the blooms are of such perfect symmetry and of such a lovely shade of old rose that it should still be grown.

White Selfs

AVALANCHE   A grand exhibition white of great purity, the bloom being held on long rigid stems.

BOOKHAM SPICE   Probably the best border white ever introduced. The flowers are of perfect formation and possess great substance.

SNOW CLOVE   A pure white of exhibition form and having a powerful clove perfume.

White Ground Fancy

BOOKHAM DANDY   The pure white blooms are marked with wide stripes of crimson-red.

BOOKHAM DREAM   A giant both in its constitution and in the size of its bloom, which is of pure white, heavily marked with scarlet.

BOOKHAM LAD   The large white blooms are heavily striped with scarlet to give a most striking effect.

DOROTHY ROBINSON   A fine exhibitor's border, the perfectly shaped blooms being heavily splashed with rosy-red.

DUSKY MAID   Bears a bloom of great substance, the white ground being heavily marked with deepest crimson, giving it quite a dusky appearance.

FANCY FREE   Has achieved fame on the show bench for the exquisite smoothness of its petals which are white, edged and marked with rose.

ISOBEL KENNEDY   The blooms are large and of perfect form and are heavily marked with crimson-red.

Yellow Selfs

BEAUTY OF CAMBRIDGE   An old favourite but should still be grown for its smoothness of petal, perfect symmetry and pure sulphur-yellow colouring.

BOOKHAM QUEEN   Outstanding in its section, the clear lemon-yellow blooms being held on rigid stems.

BOOKHAM SUN   A real exhibitor's plant, the buttercup-yellow blooms radiating intense brightness and being of perfect form.

DAFFODIL   A new border yellow of vigorous habit, its perfectly formed flowers being of bright canary-yellow.

Yellow Ground Fancies

ARGOSY   A fine old favourite, the clear yellow blooms being edged and marked with scarlet.

BOOKHAM FANCY   A novelty, the ground colour being clear, bright yellow, edged and ticked with purple.

BOOKHAM PRINCE   Of unusual colouring, the ground being of deep amber, heavily edged and marked with crimson.

CELIA   A beauty, the ground colour of moonlight yellow being marked with bright rose-pink.

GOSHAWK   An exhibitor's variety, the large blooms, borne on stiff stems, being of bright yellow, edged and barred with violet.

KATHLEEN BROOKS   Of perfect form and extremely free-flowering, the ground colour is canary yellow, edged and striped with scarlet.

LIEUTENANT DOUGLAS   One of the best of all borders for the show bench, the blooms being large and of deep yellow marked with blood red.

THE MACINTOSH   An unusual variety, the ground colour is straw yellow, each petal being covered with spots and stripes of scarlet.

Purple, Grey and Lilac Selfs

ALBATROSS   A grey self of exquisite form, the petals having a velvet-like appearance and being overlaid with a silver sheen.

BODACH GLAS   It bears a large beautifully formed bloom of lavender-grey.

CLARABELLE   Probably the best grey, having broad velvety petals, its blooms being held on long, sturdy stems.

GREYLAG   It makes a dwarf, compact plant and is most strikingly planted with 'Highlander', with its blooms of pink and heliotrope. The dark grey blooms, held on sturdy stems, have an attractive silver sheen.

Fancies

AFTON WATER   Of bushy habit and possessing a sturdy stem. The blooms are of a bright rose, splashed with madder, producing a brilliant effect.

BONNIE LESLEY   It bears exhibition blooms of great beauty, being of a deep apricot colour, heavily suffused with brilliant scarlet.

BOOKHAM HEROINE   This is one of the finest borders in cultivation bearing a profusion of large blooms of exhibition form. The base of the petals is shrimp-pink shading out to deep cherry-red.

DOUGLAS FANCY   The most striking of all the fancies. The habit is robust, the blooms of excellent formation and the colour a vivid rose-orange, edged rich crimson-red.

EBOR   An old favourite unsurpassed for colour. The ground is chocolate, striped vivid red and deep maroon, with the bloom perfect in form.

FANCY MONARCH   A brilliant introduction of huge size and perfect habit. The ground is dusky peach, speckled and edged with the nearest shade of blue possible.

LESLIE RENNISON   A lovely bedding variety. The flowers are small but of perfect shape; the colour pansy-purple, overlaid rosy-pink.

MARY LIVINGSTONE   Introduced in recent years, of bushy habit with blooms over 3in in diameter. The colour is pansy-violet, flaked rich crimson.

ORPHEUS   It bears one of the most striking blooms of all borders, being rich coppery-orange, flaked with blue-grey.

Violets

'That which above
all yields the sweetest smell in the air is the violet.'

SIR FRANCIS BACON

As long ago as 1000 BC the violet had become the symbol of ancient Athens and throughout the western world it has been held in great esteem ever since. But the violet which modern flower lovers know will be the scentless 'Governor Herrick', grown in large numbers by commercial growers because it is so free-flowering and is in no way troubled by pest and disease. Yet we miss others of great beauty. Those who know the variety 'John Raddenbury', which bears flowers of china-blue on long stems, and the early-flowering 'Coeur d'Alsace' with its rose-pink blooms, both of which are sweetly scented, will have come to appreciate two gems amongst the spring flowers.

When you have seen these two lovely plants in bloom you will want to collect other choice and more rare violets. Certainly no garden flower possesses greater charm or a more delicious fragrance. Indeed, the violet is cleistogamos, the flowers being self-fertilising. In spring the blooms are sweetly scented but then rarely set seed, whilst in autumn the blooms are much smaller, possess little fragrance but set some seed.

From earliest times violet blooms have been used as a cure for sleeplessness and as a sweetmeat. In the *Little Herball*, written in 1525, Anthony Ascham had this to say; 'for they that may not sleep, seep this herb in water, and at eventide let him soak well his feet in the water to the ancles and when he goeth to bed, bind of this herb to the temples, and he shall sleep well by the Grace of God'.

The blooms, dried and crystallised, have been used for cake decoration and as a sweetmeat since mediaeval times. Today they are used to decorate chocolates containing a violet-flavoured cream. Candied violets are made by dipping the flower heads in a solution of gum arabic and rose water, then sprinkling with fine sugar. They are placed in a slightly warm oven to dry.

For centuries, violets have been sold in the streets of London and of other towns and cities, but surprisingly almost all the cut bloom was imported from France, the rest reaching the cities from the countryside. Commercially, the crop is generally confined to the south-west, where the damp, warm climate proves ideal for the crop and where winter blooms may be enjoyed without the aid of glass. But this does not mean that the violet will not grow well elsewhere. In the home garden, it may be made to grow almost anywhere, provided it is given the conditions it enjoys, and though the bloom, in exposed gardens, may not be very early, it will be just as much appreciated when it appears. The plants must also be confined to those districts which are free of heavy industry as they will not tolerate a polluted atmosphere.

Situation

Violets will provide a charming appearance used in small beds about the garden, whilst for a rockery many varieties will be equally suitable. The ideal position should be one where the plants receive some shade from the summer sun and protection from winter and spring winds. Enjoying exactly the same conditions as the strawberry, for both are plants of the hedgerow and deciduous woodlands, the two may be grown together.

To provide shade from the summer sun does not mean that violets should be planted in the permanent shade given by buildings, or by a shrubbery planted with evergreens such as laurels, where violets are so often grown in private gardens. Such conditions will prove unsuitable, for to deprive the plants entirely of spring sunshine will mean that they will bear little bloom, and the health of the plants will rapidly deteriorate. Likewise where planting too close to a hedge, the plants will be deprived of essential food and moisture. Planting in beds between orchard trees, whereby the plants receive all possible winter and spring sunshine until the trees come into bloom in May, will prove ideal, also where planting is done in the partial shade of small deciduous trees in the home garden. To make up a bed several feet away from a tall hedge, preferably on the southern side of the land, whereby it will provide shade for the plants during midsummer, will also prove a suitable site. If a study is made of the natural environment of the violet, it will be found that it will select a more shaded position than the *Viola tricolor*, the parent of our modern pansies and violas. Thus the cultivated sweet violet prefers a more sheltered position than either the pansy or viola, but if the plants are deprived of winter and spring sunshine the valuable early bloom will be long delayed.

Soil Preparation

Of equal importance in the selection of a suitable position for the plants will be the preparation of the soil. For the violet, a soil retentive of summer moisture, yet which is well drained in winter, is essential to healthy, vigorous plant growth, resulting in an abundance of bloom. With its slight acid reaction, peat is a most suitable form of humus for violets, and should be liberally incorporated into heavy and light soils. Where the soil is of a medium loam, lucky indeed is the grower, for it will require only limited quantities of humus. The humus should be incorporated to a depth of at least 12in, for violets are deep-rooting plants and search deeply for moisture and food. Soil which does not retain moisture through the dry summer months will never grow good violets, however much plant food is available.

In addition to humus, the plants, to bloom freely and over a long period, must have ample supplies of food. As with all members of the family, in-organic plant food must never be used where there is not sufficient humus in the soil. Even so, better than any other form of fertiliser is farmyard manure, which is thoroughly decayed.

Where farmyard manure is difficult to obtain, work into the soil liberal quantities of used hops, seaweed or shoddy, in addition to the peat or leaf mould. The ground should be cleared of all perennial weeds at the same time, and just before planting a dressing of 1oz per square yard of sulphate of potash should be given, or a liberal application of wood ash which has been stored in a dry condition and which will contain liberal supplies of potash. It should be said that though violets enjoy best a soil of a slightly acid nature, they will not be happy in an unduly acid soil, yet another reason why violets so often fail in town gardens. Where growing under town conditions, or where the soil is of a too acid nature, it should be dressed with lime during the winter prior to planting in spring.

Planting

The runners should be set out during April and May, when the soil is in a friable condition, and preferably whilst the weather is showery. They should be planted 12 to 15in apart depending upon the vigour of a variety. Over-crowding should be avoided, otherwise the plants will bear less bloom through using up nutrition in the soil too quickly. Too close planting may also cause an outbreak of mildew during a period of humid weather.

From mid-July, plants should be given a weekly application of dilute manure water, which is best given during a showery day, or failing this it should be well watered in, so that the manurial value reaches the roots.

Immediately after the first application of fertiliser, the plants should be given a mulch. This will help to retain moisture in the soil during the height of summer, besides keeping down weeds. It will be amazing how well the plants respond to a feed and a mulch, an abundance of new growth appearing as if by magic. The closer to the plants the peat mulch is given, the better they will respond, and by the end of summer when the plants are ready for the frames, or for covering where they have been planted in the open, they will have made large clumps composed of a number of crowns, and in consequence cannot fail to give an abundance of bloom. Peat mixed with a small quantity of decayed manure, especially cow manure, will prove excellent as a mulch. Old mushroom bed compost is valuable. Spent hops and bark fibre may also be used. After the mulch has been given, hoeing should stop, for by then the plants will have made considerable growth, and their roots will be reaching out to a considerable distance, and may be damaged if hoeing is done too close to the plants. In any case, the mulch will do the work of the hoe.

The amateur could use a mixture of peat, decayed manure and loam with which to mulch the plants, and an occasional dusting of the soil with weathered

Old-fashioned flowers grow in profusion in a Cambridgeshire cottage garden

soot will prove a splendid tonic. If only the plants were frequently divided and planted into fresh ground and could be given a mulch in summer, there would be few of those shy or non-flowering plants to be found in so many gardens. Small growers could well use leaf mould for mulching, for it is in this that the violet of our woodlands propagates itself by runners and maintains its health. Throughout summer the aim must be to keep the plants growing healthily. In a dry season, mulch and water frequently, and during a wet summer fortify the plants with regular applications of fertiliser, especially potash. Plants which come to a standstill will never bear an abundance of bloom when most required, whilst they will be prone to all manner of troubles.

Remember to shade the plants whenever necessary by erecting canvas, or hurdles, where the plants are growing in an open situation, and remove all runners as they appear. Those suitable may be rooted in frames or in a shady border, whilst any which may have formed roots can be planted in beds or rows to come into bloom late in spring.

After the plants have flowered, they may be grown-on for a second year if they remain healthy. Where this is to be done, quite a good idea is to treat them similarly to second-year strawberries. The three or four runners nearest the parent plants are pegged down around the plants after the ground has been weeded. This will give the beds almost a mat-like appearance, and make further cultivations almost impossible. Plant growth will, however, keep down weeds and provided the plants are given regular applications of manure water throughout the summer, both old and new plants should give a good account of themselves the following winter and spring. They will be better allowed to bloom without glass protection. Afterwards, the plants should be cleared and destroyed and the ground allowed to remain idle into the late autumn, when it may be prepared for planting in the following spring.

Propagation

The violet may be propagated in numerous ways but is chiefly increased by removal of runners which will have rooted whilst still attached to the parent plants, it being a simple matter to detach them and make up new beds whenever required.

The first runners will be ready for removal in early spring immediately after plants in frames have finished flowering; or where plants have been flowering out of doors, the first runners will have formed during April and May. Not all will be suitable for propagation and only those which form a rosette or cluster of leaves along the string should be used for reproduction. Those which form only an odd leaf or so, rather than a crown, will never make suitable flowering plants and should be destroyed. It will be found that the strings or runners will have formed roots along the underside portion of the stem, and beneath the rosette or crown, so that they should be removed with about an inch of the string. This will help the rosette to grow away vigorously, and especially will the additional rootlets prove useful during a dry period. Runners removed in spring will grow into plants suitable for removing to cold frames in September, and in the more favourable districts these same plants will come into bloom in the early weeks of the winter.

Elsewhere, the plants are grown-on outdoors until the following spring, when they will come into bloom in March in the normal way. It will be advisable to remove any flower buds which appear during the summer and all runners must be removed as they form. A plant required to bear large quantities of bloom during winter and early spring cannot be expected to be allowed to reproduce itself at the same time. If allowed to do so, then it will bear less bloom. So as to obtain as large a number of rooted runners as possible from those plants which have flowered, rooting will be hastened and will be more reliable if some of the strings are pegged down with carnation layering pins, though generally there will be large numbers that will root without any help whatsoever.

Propagation in this way may continue throughout summer, at all times keeping the soil thoroughly moist about the plants, which should be partially covered with a mixture of peat and soil, or with leaf mould, when they will form additional runners with renewed vigour which may be removed until the middle of September.

Unrooted runners from young plants which have been set out in spring should be removed as they appear. They should either be planted in cold frames, where they will quickly root, or where they may have already formed rootlets. Make up into beds outdoors, spacing the plants 4 to 5in apart. At the end of summer every third plant should be removed to form a new bed, the others remaining to bloom in early spring.

The time when the runners are removed will determine the flowering time of the plants. Those removed in early spring will come into bloom in October in the south, or early in spring in the less favourable districts. When removed between June and October, either from the old plants or from runners set out in early spring, they will bloom later; in the south early in spring, in the north during late spring. Provided some runners are removed during March and April, to build up into sturdy plants to bloom in winter, additional beds should be made up with later runners and cuttings, to provide bloom when those growing in frames or outdoors early in spring are coming to an end. In this way heavy pickings will continue from the early winter months until well into May.

Use of Cloches

Plants may be covered with cloches, to bloom from October whenever weather conditions permit, whilst with the spring flowering varieties, or where it is required to have large pickings in spring, cloches may be used to cover the plants early in February. The more southerly growers find only limited use for cloches, but where early spring bloom is required in the colder districts, cloches will prove indispensable and will permit out-of-season bloom to be enjoyed with the minimum of labour and expense.

Where barn-type cloches are to be used for covering the plants, they should be set out in single rows in the ordinary way as when growing by the row system, rather than in beds. The same remarks appertain to plants which are to come into bloom in early autumn, and are to be covered with cloches, as for those grown in frames. They must be propagated as early in spring as possible to enable them to enjoy a long season to build themselves up into sturdy plants. A number of varieties lend themselves more to cloche culture than others by way of their compact habit. This not only reduces the incidence of mildew but enables slightly closer planting to be done in the rows. It must be said, however, that too close planting, the aim being to get as many plants as possible under cover, will most probably cause trouble. Varieties suitable for cloche culture are 'California', 'Coeur d'Alsace', 'Mrs Lloyd George', 'Princess Alexandra', 'Luxonne' and *semperflorens*.

It will be of the utmost importance to keep the glass of the cloches perfectly clean, washing with soapy water before the plants are covered. To provide ventilation, cloches should be removed at regular intervals along the rows on all suitable days. If the weather continues dry for any length of time the cloches should be removed and the plants syringed and the soil given a thorough soaking. Every so often the plants should be completely uncovered to allow them to receive gentle rain. Though the plants must be treated as hardy as far as possible, the cloches should be in position during wet and misty weather, also during periods of hard frost. It is advisable to keep the plants covered just before a flush of bloom is ready to be gathered, whilst any spraying or dusting for pest and disease attack should always be done between flushes of bloom.

Varieties

Single

ADMIRAL AVELLAN   This old variety remains one of the best of all violets. The blooms are large, freely produced and are of a rich reddish-purple colour, whilst they are amongst the most strongly scented of all violets. The plant is extremely hardy and seems to do well in all soils and in all districts, coming early into bloom and continuing late.

ASKANIA   An excellent flower, bearing a long pointed bloom of a lovely shade of true violet. Not quite as hardy as some, it flourishes freely under glass and possesses a powerful fragrance. The blooms are held on long, wiry stems.

BOURNEMOUTH GEM   Due to its resistance to red spider this new variety is rapidly gaining in popularity. It is extremely free-flowering, the blooms being of a rich purple-blue colour. The blooms possess slight perfume where grown in a cool, moist climate, elsewhere none at all.

CALIFORNIA   The rich violet-purple blooms are held on long stems. The blooms are of beautiful form with pointed upper petals and they carry a rich perfume. An excellent variety for cloche culture and for the open ground, for it is quite hardy.

COEUR D'ALSACE   A charming old variety which blooms extremely well under glass during winter, bearing its sweetly perfumed rose-pink blooms on long stems. Though not a popular commercial variety, it should be in every amateur gardener's collection. The first to open its blooms in the open and excellent for a rockery.

GOVERNOR HERRICK   Though being completely devoid of any perfume, the plants are so resistant to pest and disease as to make this the most popular variety with present-day commercial growers. The blooms, freely produced, are large and handsome and are of a bright purple-blue colour. Does well on shallow chalk soil.

JOHN RADDENBURY   This little-known variety is one of the loveliest of all violets, the blooms being bright china-blue, sweetly perfumed and held on long, sturdy stems. In certain soils the blooms may have a rose flush. Should be more widely grown for market, for the bloom sells well.

LUXONNE   An extremely hardy violet, not nearly so well known as it deserves to be. It is very resistant to pest and disease and ever prolific. The large blooms, held on long sturdy stems, are almost of a true shade of navy blue.

MADAM SCHWARTZ   For northern violet lovers this is one of the hardiest varieties, for it will come into bloom quite unprotected early in March and earlier if the weather is kind. The blooms are large and of a bright shade of violet-blue, borne on long stems.

MRS DAVID LLOYD GEORGE   This old blue violet with its striking pale yellow centre may be classed as a semi-double variety and is one of the best of all. The blooms, borne on long thick stems, carry a sweet woodland perfume, and are freely produced during winter, given the protection of glass. Also known as 'Cyclops' on account of its eye or centre.

MRS F. W. DWIGHT   This is a new introduction of excellent quality which blooms well under glass and is free-flowering outdoors. The large violet-blue flowers are borne on tall, erect stems over a long period.

PRINCESS OF WALES   But for its susceptibility to red spider this would be the most popular of all violets with the commercial grower. It is very free-flowering, does reasonably well under glass and extremely so in the open, bearing its large rich violet-blue flowers on long stems. The blooms are similar in size and shape to *V. gracilis*, and possess a strong fragrance. The habit of the plants is robust, the blooms being borne on long, sturdy stems. It was first sent out from the gardens at Windsor Castle.

SEMPERFLORENS   Showing considerable hardiness and resistance to disease, besides flowering over a longer period than any other violet, it would be more widely grown but for the pale colouring of its purple-blue flowers, which when bunched soon appear as if slightly faded. Lovely for a rockery on account of its compact habit.

SULPHUREA   This is the only yellow-coloured violet, and though it may not be a favourite with the public so that little planted commercially, it is a delightful plant in the garden. Its compact habit is ideal for the rockery, whilst in partial shade its brightly coloured blooms reveal their true beauty. The blooms are not a true yellow, rather a Jersey cream colour, flushed with apricot-buff. A form called 'Irish Elegance' bears a bloom of a slightly deeper shade of cream-buff. The blooms carry a pleasing woodland fragrance, and whilst the plants bear well under glass, *V. sulphurea* cannot be considered as free as some.

VICTORIA REGINA   Valuable for cloche culture in that it makes a tiny, neat plant, yet comes early into bloom and flowers profusely. The blooms are large, delicately perfumed and are a bright violet-blue.

Double

COUNTESS OF SHAFTESBURY   Free-flowering and of vigorous habit, and reasonably hardy, it bears one of the loveliest of all semi-double violet blooms, the colour being pale lavender-blue with rose-pink centre petals and attractive green stamens. The blooms, borne on strong, erect stems, carry a delicate, sweet fragrance.

LADY HUME CAMPBELL   With 'Marie Louise' this is one of the finest of all varieties for cloche culture, and possesses additional value in that it is the last of the doubles to come into bloom and so extends the season. It is also one of the hardiest of the doubles and with 'Mrs J. J. Astor' is perhaps the most free-flowering. The plant is of vigorous habit and bears a bloom of an attractive shade of lavender-blue.

MADEMOISELLE BERTHA BARRON   A hardy variety of strong, vigorous habit, though forming a compact plant, making it ideal for under-glass culture. It bears a deep purple-blue flower which is sweetly scented, though not too freely produced.

MRS ARTHUR   Hardier and more free-flowering than 'Marie Louise', which the bloom closely resembles in colour and form, though it is not so sweetly perfumed. It is an excellent variety for cloche culture, for which it is widely planted commercially, in fact, it does well anywhere and may be classed as one of the easiest of the doubles.

MRS J. J. ASTOR   Extremely free-flowering, either in the open or under glass, the very double flowers are of a distinct shade of rose-pink. The blooms, held on erect stems, possess a powerful fragrance. Away from the south-west should be given under-glass culture.

Pansies and Violas

'. . . like a miniature cat's face gazing up at me.'

WILLIAM THOMPSON

Compared with the auricula and double primrose, well known to Tudor gardeners, the pansy and viola are modern flowers, in their present form being found in our gardens for little more than a century. The modern Show and Fancy pansies are far removed from Shakespeare's Love-in-Idleness, Viola *tricolor* of the higher meadowlands and *V. lutea*, which Parkinson, botanist to Charles I, called the Great Yellow Pansy. It was this latter form which William Thompson, gardener to Lord Gambier at Iver, used in raising the first pansies with the now familiar blotches which he introduced in 1839. The first variety was called 'Thompson's King' and this was followed by 'Thompson's Medora', which the raiser found in a bed of seedlings: 'like a miniature cat's face gazing up at me'.

The cooler climate of the North proved more suitable to the culture of these new pansies, and by 1850 Scottish gardeners were exhibiting these new pansies which flourished and bloomed to perfection under the cool conditions.

Show Pansies

The Show pansy may be divided into two classes, the belted or margined bi-colours and self colours. The blooms should be smooth and circular, with no waviness in the petals, whilst they should be of velvet-like appearance. The eye should be small, whilst the two centre petals should meet above the eye and reach well up the top petals. The lower petals should be deep and broad to balance the others, the top of these lower petals being horizontal with the two centre petals arranged evenly on either side of an imaginary perpendicular line drawn through the eye.

As to the correct markings of the margined pansies, the ground colour should be the same throughout, with the margin well defined and of uniform width and of the same colour as the two upper petals. The blotches should be as near circular as possible with the eye well defined and of a bright yellow colour.

The self colours may again be divided into dark- and light-coloured varieties, the upper and lower petals being of the same colour and free from any blotch. The same remarks as to petal form and texture apply.

A coloured engraving of pansies, 1849: (*left*) 'Mrs Beck' and (*right*) 'Duke of Norfolk'

Varieties

ALICE RUTHERFORD   A deep yellow self of fine form.

BLUE BELL   A dark blue self of great beauty.

CHAS. MCCRERIE   A margined variety, the ground colour is sulphur-yellow with a violet margin.

GOLDEN GIFT   The ground colour is deep yellow with a belting of violet.

JAMES GRAME   A beauty, the ground colour being deep cream, the belting and upper petals rich purple.

JAMES THOM   The ground is brilliant golden-yellow, the belting and upper petals being of chocolate colouring.

MRS RUTH THOMPSON   The ground colour is primrose-yellow, the margin and upper petals being rosy-mauve.

Fancy Pansies

The Fancy pansies were widely grown on the Continent during the mid-nineteenth century and became known as Belgian pansies, the blooms being circular, with smooth, velvet-like petals lying evenly over each other. Here, there is no definition as to colours, but the blotch of violet or chocolate colour should almost cover the whole of the three lower petals with the exception of a wide margin which may be of any colour or of more than one colour. The upper petals need not be the same colour as the margin and may be of rose, cream, purple, gold or intermediate shades. It is thus possible to obtain some brilliantly coloured blooms.

Varieties

ADAM WHITE   The large blotches are of chocolate colouring, the edges and top petals being of golden-yellow, suffused with violet.

ALDERLEY   A Jackson introduction, the refined blooms having large circular blotches of deep plum, the lower petals being margined rosy-pink. The upper petals are white, flushed with purple and edged white.

ALEX LISTER   The dense blotches are of chocolate colouring, the edges rose and cream with the top petals rosy-purple.

ANNIE LISTER   The bloom has a large almost black blotch and a margin of cream. The upper petals are violet-mauve, with a broad margin of cream.

BETTY SHEPPARD   A favourite variety having a large black blotch and clearly defined margins of vivid yellow.

CATHERINE   The blotches are violet, the edges ruby, with the upper petals a rich shade of purple.

DR MCKINNON   Has violet blotches, the petals being edged with cream, with the upper petals cream and rosy-violet.

ENA WHITELAW   Its blotches are chocolate-coloured, the petals being edged with gold, with the upper petals soft purple.

ERNEST CHEETHAM   A magnificent new variety of great size with deep plum blotches and a narrow edging of white round the lower petals, the upper petals being plum coloured.

GEORGE CLOSE   A lovely pansy, the blotches are parma-violet with margins of old rose.

HENRY STIRLING   The bloom is huge with a chocolate-coloured blotch and belting of yellow flushed with crimson. The top petals are yellow, margined with crimson.

JAMES MCMURTRIE   The blotches are dark brown, the lower petals being margined with yellow. The upper petals are yellow, suffused light blue.

JANET NORRIS   A most striking variety, having deep purple blotches with a thin margin of ivory round the lower petals.

JESSIE BISHOP   A new variety, the large blooms having a jet-black blotch and margins of deep mahogany.

MRS A. B. COCHRANE   A huge bloom with purple blotches and cream margins; the upper petals being purple and cream.

MRS CAMPBELL   A yellow self with huge circular claret-coloured blotches.

MRS H. CHEETHAM   The huge blooms have velvet-purple blotches and pale lemon-yellow margins.

MRS PUGH   A striking flower with crimson blotches and wide deep yellow margins.

NEIL MCCOLL   The blotches are plum, the lower petals being margined with rose and white. The top petals are cream and purple.

SUSAN   The refined blooms have mahogany blotches with chrome-yellow margins.

T. B. COCHRANE   Dark blue blotches, the lower petals being margined white, with the top petals purple and white.

W. B. CHILD   A variety of refined form having a huge purple blotch with a margin of gold. The upper petals are deep golden yellow with purple blotches.

WILLIAM WHYTE   The enormous blooms have deep velvet-purple blotches and cream margins.

Culture

The plants like plenty of moisture and cool conditions about their roots. All too often pansies are planted in a position of full sun and in a soil devoid of humus. The result is that they finish flowering all too soon, and if the summer is unduly dry, the plants may prove but short-lived. They will also fail to bear a bloom of the quality and size to be obtained where some humus has been provided. Where this has not been given at planting time, work in some thoroughly decayed manure, especially cow manure, peat or bark fibre, placing it about the crown of the plant, and to prolong the display a second mulching should be given during August. An occasional feeding of diluted liquid blood or manure water will also enhance the display.

Second-season plants which come into bloom early in summer will benefit from cutting back, towards the end of July, all shoots to within 2in of the base. Vigorous new growth will soon appear and the display will be continued until autumn, or the new shoots may be removed for rooting.

Young plants which have been blooming freely will benefit from the removal of all buds for ten days during July, so as to give the plants a rest. They will come again with renewed vigour. Mulching should be done at the same time. After the season has ended, all shoots should be again shortened and some humus forked around the plants. This will not only keep the plants neat and tidy but will ensure them a long life. During a dry summer it is important to keep pansies thoroughly moist about the roots, whilst the foliage will also benefit from a regular syringing with clean water.

To keep the plants clear of green fly, the most troublesome pest of the pansy and viola, spray once every ten days with Lindex, a quarter fluid ounce dissolved in a gallon of water, and particularly allow it to reach the underside of the leaves. Also never allow the dead blooms to remain on the plants and form seed, otherwise the plants will soon finish flowering.

To propagate the named varieties, cut back all long or old shoots and remove the short cuttings at a leaf joint as they appear from the base. This may be done during July, after the first flush of bloom has finished, and until early autumn, the cuttings being inserted into a frame or into boxes containing a sand and peat compost which must be kept comfortably moist. The cuttings should be shaded from the direct rays of the sun whilst to prevent mildew, dust the cuttings with flowers of sulphur. They will root in a month, when they should be planted out into beds to bloom the following summer, or they may be allowed to remain in the frames over winter for planting out in March.

The cuttings should be taken from only one variety at a time and these should be inserted in rows or in sections, clearly named.

Exhibiting

Where growing for exhibition, timing is all important, and to ensure an adequate supply of blooms on show day, all bloom should be removed fifteen days prior to the show, for this is the length of time it takes a new bud to develop and reach perfection.

Pansies resent strong sunshine and, if growing for exhibition in an exposed position, the bloom should be protected from the sun's rays by placing a short stake close to the plant and fixing to the top a square of cardboard to almost cover the plant 2 to 3in above the bloom. Also, to prevent the blooms falling over and becoming splashed by heavy rains, it is advisable to stake each shoot where the blooms are required for exhibition. Damp newspaper placed around the plants will also prevent splashing and act as a mulch.

As soon as the buds are fully open, great care must be taken with watering for they so easily become marked. When removing the bloom for exhibition,

break or cut the stalk at the point where it joins the shoot, place in a small jar of water and remove to a cool room without delay, never at any time touching the bloom with the fingers or it may bruise.

To arrange the blooms for display, they are placed in small glass test tubes, their stems being fastened together in sprays by wires and lengths of wool which will suck up the moisture and keep the blooms fresh. To remove them to the show, the tubes are placed in buckets of sand.

A most attractive table display for the home may be arranged by fastening the blooms to the wires with green wool and placing them in a bowl of moist sand to which a little moist peat has been added. They may be arranged in fan-like form, and if the sand is kept damp the blooms will remain fresh for fully a week.

Violas

The 'Father of the bedding viola' was James Grieve of apple fame, who crossed *V. lutea* and *V. cornuta,* which had been introduced from Spain in 1776, with the show and fancy pansies. The result was a plant of more perennial habit, with greater freedom of flowering. Most violas, too, have a compact habit and thus are more suitable for bedding.

Where building up a collection, the plants may be placed in sections by the side of a path or drive, using contrasting colours, or they may be used to border rose-beds or beds of any other flowering plants. Large quantities of viola plants may be raised possibly for selling by planting in special stock-beds and rooting the cuttings taken from the base of the plants during the latter weeks of summer and early in autumn. They are rooted in frames as previously described for pansies, or, where rooting in July, beds may be made up unprotected, possibly beneath a northerly wall.

To make up a small bed beneath a wall and where the cuttings will not receive the full rays of the mid-day sun, a length of 9in boarding at the front and held in place by wooden pegs will give protection from cold winds.

To obtain sturdy cuttings, remove only the basal shoots, those which have not yet flowered, for shoots which have borne bloom will be hollow-stemmed and will not make suitable plants whilst being more difficult to root. Select the shoots only from healthy plants. The selected shoots should be from 2 to 3in long and may easily be nipped off with the fingers and removed to a cool room for preparation. Here they should be trimmed immediately beneath a leaf joint, the lower pair of leaves being carefully removed by pulling them in an upwards direction to prevent tearing the stem.

The exhibition fancy pansy 'Roslin'

The cuttings are dibbled into the rooting medium 3in apart, but do not plant so deeply that the lower leaves will rest on the soil or mildew may occur. Make them quite firm, water them in and dust with green flowers of sulphur to guard against mildew. Should the weather be sunny, it will be advisable to shield them from the sun's rays until roots have formed. The cuttings will appreciate a syringing with clean water whenever the weather is warm, but provide some ventilation so that excess moisture will be evaporated. The cuttings should have formed a thick bunch of roots within a month, when the frame lights (or cloches) may be removed until the advent of winter, or until required for planting out. Never at any time allow the young plants to suffer from lack of moisture.

Violas enjoy similar cultural conditions to the pansy, though they will tolerate a soil containing rather less humus. Decayed manure, used hops, peat and bark fibre will be suitable materials to work into the soil, for the more friable and moist soil conditions become, the more perennial will be the plants, remaining vigorous and free-flowering for several years.

The viola, or tufted pansy, may be divided into two sections, quite apart from the numerous hybrids grown from seed: varieties suitable for exhibition and those used for bedding. It may generally be assumed that exhibition varieties are those which bear a larger and more refined flower, yet not all of such form come within the requirements set down by the various societies. The bloom should be circular, with the petals lying evenly over each other. The centre petals should meet above the eye, whilst the lower petals should be deep and broad, to give balance to the bloom. The colour may be self, mottled, suffused or margined, but must be entirely free of any blotch or rays. Thus, of the more popular varieties, whilst 'Moseley Perfection' with its refined golden-yellow bloom, entirely rayless, may be used on the show bench, 'Bullion', which is extremely free-flowering and of similar, though slightly richer colour, would not be accepted for exhibition, for the bloom is anything but refined in form and it is heavily rayed. As with all show pansies and violas the eye must be bright and clearly defined, whilst the bloom must be more than $2\frac{1}{2}$in in diameter. Flowers which have gaps between the petals or where the petals are thin at the edges, also where the eye is too large, will not be suitable for exhibition. Colour is given greater prominence, by those judging, than any other point, and a bloom which tends to fade, or with margined varieties, where this is ill-defined, will fail to win maximum points.

Exhibition Varieties

ADA JACKSON Quite a new colour break. The large white blooms have a medium edge of rosy-mauve on the three lower petals, the upper petals being suffused rosy-mauve.

AGNES COCHRANE The lower petals are crimson-purple, the top petals rich mauve splashed with purple.

ANDREW JACKSON   Its refined bloom is of a rich shade of purple, striped with amethyst and pale mauve.

A. S. FRATER   The large blooms of this excellent variety are creamy white and margined with mauve.

BARBARA BENNETT   A crimson-purple self of massive, but refined, form.

C. S. ROBERTSON   A pure cream self of excellent form.

DORA MCGILL   A plum self of great size and substance.

ELIZABETH WILLIAMS   The huge blooms are of deep mauve with an attractive cream centre.

HELEN COCHRANE   Possibly the finest pure white yet raised.

H. H. HODGE   Has a lemon ground with a wire edge of lavender. Excellent habit.

JOHN ADAMSON   A grand pure golden-yellow.

KATHLEEN HAYLE   A pure cream self of lovely form.

LADY TENNYSON   The habit of this outstanding pure white is ideal in every way.

MARY ANDERSON   An outstanding viola, the pale sulphur-yellow blooms are edged with mauve.

MAY CHEETHAM   This superb new variety is likely to be the most popular viola of its colour on the show bench for many years. The huge bloom is pure primrose-yellow, rayless and of great substance.

MAY JACKSON   The primrose-yellow lower petals are edged with mauve, the upper petals suffused mauve.

MILNER'S FANCY   Its bloom is large and of deep purple-red, striped with rose.

MOSELEY IDEAL   Large blooms of palest cream, edged with mauve.

MOSELEY PERFECTION   The beautifully formed golden-yellow blooms are entirely rayless.

MRS A. BLEARS   An exceptional variety, the pale cream blooms have a wire edge of purple.

MRS A. COCHRANE   Large blooms with a cream centre and edged and suffused pale lavendar.

MRS A. STEVENSON   The large flowers are pale yellow, suffused at the edges with heliotrope.

MRS J. H. LITTLE   Has primrose-yellow blooms, heavily banded with an unusual slate-blue colour.

MRS J. ROBERTSON   The sulphur-yellow blooms have an attractive picotee edge of lavender. The top petals are also pencilled lavender.

MRS M. WALLACE   Unusual in that the bloom is lavender, speckled or marbled with purple.

MRS T. BATES   A fine pure yellow self of lovely form.

PEACE   One of the finest of all exhibition violas but now rarely to be seen. The large circular rayless blooms are creamy-white, slightly flushed with lavender.

PICKERING BLUE   A most popular viola for exhibition and bedding. The large, sweetly scented blooms are of a shade of deep sky-blue.

R. N. DENBY   An outstanding variety, the pale lemon-yellow bloom being edged with pale blue.

ROBERT WEBB   A dark-flowered blue 'sport' from 'Pickering Blue', and possessing the same excellent qualities.

ROWAN HOOD   The large well-formed blooms are deep chrome-yellow, belted with lavender.

SUE STEVENSON   One of the finest varieties ever raised, both for exhibition and bedding. The large blooms are of a rich shade of violet with a large clear yellow centre.

SUSAN   A new viola for exhibition; a seedling from the popular 'Ada Jackson'. The white bloom has a margin of mid-blue on the lower petals, the top petals being suffused blue.

WILLIAM JACKSON   The refined blooms are brilliant golden-yellow with a picotee edge of white.

Bedding Violas

The qualities of a bedding viola are that the plants should possess a dwarf, compact habit, and should be free-flowering, the flower stem to be erect and of sufficient length to maintain the blooms above the foliage. Where used for exhibition, the blooms should be, like the Exhibition varieties, quite free of rays and blotches, though this generally adds to their attraction when used for garden display.

It should be said that the viola in all its forms is always more satisfactory in the south than is the pansy, proving better able to withstand warmer and drier conditions. For this reason, the viola has increased in popularity to the exclusion of the true show and fancy pansy. William Robinson, who did so much to popularise the viola, has written that in the south the margined varieties such as 'Goldfinch' and 'Duchess of Fife' were never as reliable as the self-colours, for their margins were never so clearly defined as where growing in the north. There is some degree of truth in this statement, though modern varieties are more reliable in this respect, whilst planting in partial shade will do much to provide the cool conditions which all members of the family love best.

Bedding Varieties

ADMIRAL OF THE BLUES   A fine old exhibition variety, now used chiefly for bedding. The mid-blue flowers, suffused with crimson and a striking yellow eye, make this one of the best violas ever introduced.

AMY BARR   A fine bedding variety. The blooms are deep pink with a white centre.

'Woodsmoor', a white viola, edged with pale blue

ARABELLA   The bloom of this most beautiful viola is pale mauve, deepening to violet at the edges.

BLUESTONE   An extremely old variety of most compact habit. The clear mid-blue colour of the medium-sized blooms, with their golden eye surrounded by a small purple blotch, make it unbeatable for bedding. Very long in bloom.

BRENDA RUSHWORTH   An unusual variety, the large lemon-yellow blooms being flushed with lilac at the edges.

BULLION   Almost a hundred years old, and for its freedom of flowering still widely planted. Brilliant golden-yellow and rayed. Very compact and early to bloom.

CRIMSON BEDDER   The blooms are of a rich crimson-purple shade, produced with great freedom.

DOBBIE'S BRONZE   Probably the best bronze for bedding. The blooms are bright, with a terracotta flush, and with a bronze blotch at the centre.

IRISH MOLLY   The colourings are so diverse as to make it difficult to describe, but generally bronzy yellow, with a copper centre, the bloom having quite a green appearance. Of excellent habit.

JACKANAPES   A very old variety, the upper petals being crimson-brown, the lower petals bright yellow.

JAMES PILLING   A fine belted pansy, the white bloom being margined with lavender-blue.

J. B. RIDING   This 'sport' from 'Wm. Neil', is an old favourite, the bright, slightly rayed, purple blooms being produced with freedom.

KATHLEEN   The white blooms have a thick edge of reddish mauve with a mauve-pink blotch on the upper petals.

MAGGIE MOTT   Extremely long and free-flowering, bearing silvery-mauve blooms of great beauty. One of the best violas ever introduced.

MISS BROOKS   A uniquely coloured viola, the large blooms being of a deep cerise-pink self colour.

MOSELEY CREAM   The large refined blooms are of a lovely jersey cream colour.

PALMER'S WHITE   A fine white for massing. The blooms are medium-sized, the habit of the plant being most compact. Use with 'Bluestone' or 'Maggie Mott'.

PRIMROSE DAME   Extremely free-flowering, the primrose-yellow blooms have a bright golden eye.

REDBRASES BRONZE   An old variety of excellent habit, the bronzy blooms being beautifully shaded old gold.

ROYAL SOVEREIGN   Fine rayless deep yellow, similar in colour to 'Bullion', but a better shaped bloom. One of the best.

RUTH ELKINS   The large rich yellow blooms are attractively edged with deep purple-blue.

T. E. WOLSTENHOLME   A grand variety, the medium-sized bloom being of a rich chestnut-bronze colour.

WHITE SWAN   An old variety sometimes called 'Swan'. The pure white blooms are rayless and have a striking orange eye.

Violettas

Viola *cornuta*, the alpine or horned violet of the Pyrenees, was introduced into England in 1776 and was used in the breeding of the garden viola and the violettas. A fibrous rooted plant of short tufted habit with heart-shaped toothed leaves, it blooms from May until August, the pale blue flowers having an awl-shaped spur. There is also a white form, *alba*. Both bear sweetly scented flowers.

Using the tufted *V. cornuta* as the seed-bearing parent and by crossing this with a pansy called 'Blue King', Dr Stuart of Chirnside obtained a strain of rayless violas which he called violettas. Though more long flowering than any of the pansies and violas, and being of more perennial habit, it is surprising that these charming plants have never become as popular as the ordinary bedding violas. They come into bloom in April, with the primroses, and continue until the frosts. The blooms of the violettas are not rounded like the pansies and violas, but are longer and more oval in shape and are borne on stiff erect flower stems well above the foliage, even more so than violas. They are little larger than those of the cultivated violet, 'Princess of Wales', and are equally as dainty. The colours are clear, the eye bright, whilst the centre rays are absent. The blooms possess a rich vanilla-like perfume and are produced over a long period. The plants are tufted, the foliage being small, bright and short-jointed. They are extremely long lasting, and should be lifted and divided every three or four years in March. Plants up to 12in across, bearing anything up to a hundred blooms, are formed.

Varieties

ADMIRATION   The larger than usual flowers are of a rich shade of purple-violet.

BABY GRANDE   Oval-shaped blooms of an attractive pale crimson-pink colour.

BLUE CARPET   Its small blooms are a brilliant blue colour.

BUTTERCUP   One of the loveliest of all the violettas, the oval blooms being of a rich orange-yellow colour.

COMPACTUM   The pale lavender blooms have a conspicuous yellow eye.

DAWN   Lovely for planting with 'Idem Gem' or 'Jersey Gem', for the blooms are of a pale shade of primrose-yellow.

HEATHER BELL   An outstanding variety bearing a bloom of rich mauve-pink.

IDEM GEM   The very dark blue flowers are held on long stems.

JERSEY GEM   Also known as 'Blue Gem'. The dainty flowers are of a deep aniline-blue colour.

LE GRANDEUR   The blooms, which are rather larger than usual, are mid-blue.

LITTLE DAVID   Cream-coloured blooms held well above the foliage possess the rich fragrance of freesias.

LORNA   Beautiful with deep lavender-blue blooms.

PERFECTION   The dainty blooms are of a delicate shade of clear sky-blue.

QUEEN OF THE YEAR   A beautiful variety bearing small china-blue blooms.

TOM TIT   Of more recent introduction, the blooms are of a clear purple-blue shade, held well above the foliage.

VIOLETTA   The original hybrid and still obtainable. The blooms are white, suffused yellow on the lower petals, and are produced over a long period.

D. B. Crane continued with violettas where Dr Stuart had left off towards the end of the century, and amongst his finest introductions were 'Diana', with its lovely clear primrose-yellow blooms; 'Eileen', pale blue with a gold eye; and the blue and white 'Winifred Phillips'.

Stonecrops and House Leeks

'The leaves are fat, full of juice, an inch long, like little tongues, curiously minced at the edges . . .'

JOHN GERARD

These two plants may be described together, for they like much the same cultural conditions, a dry sunny situation. Both are plants which are native of north Europe and were grown on houses in ancient days, adding charm to old walls and supposedly guarding the property from lightning and witches' spells. Sedum (stonecrop) takes its name from the Latin 'to sit' for it likes to sit on stone walls with its roots in the mortar. Sempervivum (house leek) is also from the Latin *semper*, 'always' and *vivo*, 'I live' for the plants are almost indestructible. They will, in fact, grow where few other plants would survive, even in the cracks of a wall, or on the roof of an old house where their roots are able to obtain a hold onto the stone slates. All they require is a little dry soil about the roots, even some lime rubble or mortar will suffice, to provide suitable anchorage, and they are able to flourish whilst almost devoid of moisture. For planting on top of a dry wall or between crazy paving, the stonecrops are ideal plants, for many of them are of almost prostrate habit and quite apart from the diverse colouring of their foliage, which ranges from golden yellow to rich bronze, they bear tiny but colourful flowers from early summer until the end of autumn. By planting just a few of the five hundred or so different species and hybrid varieties, to be found growing about rock formation in almost every part of the world, a large area of paving could be made interesting and colourful almost the whole year round, for almost all the stonecrops are evergreen. About a sunny, exposed rockery, and indeed in any position about a garden which receives full sun and where the soil is dry and of poor quality, the stonecrops should become a subject for specialisation.

You can also specialise in house leeks. These are cactus-like in appearance with fleshy leaves which store up moisture for considerable periods, sufficient to maintain the life of the plant during long periods of drought. They make ideal plants for small pots or pans where collections may be formed in the same way as with cacti. They grow well in a sandy soil in a cold room or greenhouse, and are quite evergreen. Throughout winter especially the plants will require very little moisture and at any time of the year they may be left several weeks without attention in any way. All they require in the form of a potting compost is some fibrous loam and coarse sand in equal quantities. Add

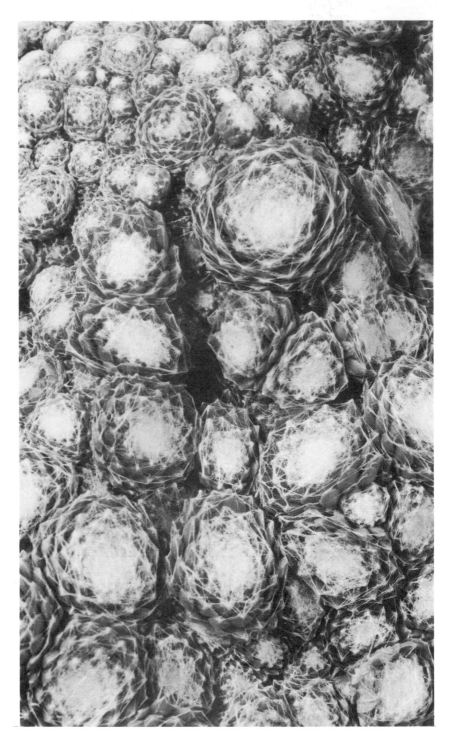

neither manure nor peat, but the plants will appreciate a little lime rubble which should be well worked into the compost.

House leeks, like the stonecrops, are not only able to survive extremely dry conditions but the brilliant colourings of their foliage are greatly enhanced by such conditions. It is, however, advisable to give the house leeks some moisture for several weeks after the plants have been potted or planted out and until they have become established. Once they have reached that point, only the very minimum of moisture necessary to keep the plants alive should be provided.

The house leeks are quite happy where planted in walls and where growing in crazy paving. About a rockery, too, they could be planted whilst a number could well be used for bedding in a sunny, exposed garden. *S. schlehanii*, for instance, makes a large rosette of fleshy leaves about 4in tall, all but the tips being stained with blood-red. The rosettes are vivid green at the centre whilst their flowers are red with striking white margins and are held on 8in stems. Imagine the rich effects that will be provided by a small bed of a dozen or so plants, being inter-planted with pale blue lobelia or white with alyssum. The house leeks may be left in the ground permanently, though where there is a small greenhouse available the plants will provide greater enjoyment if potted and taken inside in early November, when the beds may be replanted with spring-flowering plants or bulbs. Like the stonecrops, the house leeks are extremely diverse, some having incurving rosettes like a water lily in appearance, whilst others are covered with cobwebs. The colourings of the fleshy leaves range from yellow through shades of green to purple and crimson. Collections may be built up through the years and may number several hundred distinct species.

Increasing Stock

Propagation is simple. With the house leeks all that is necessary is to lift and divide the rosettes every year, or whenever spare time permits the work to be done, replant into individual pots or into pans containing just one variety. Plants to be sold are, however, best grown in 2½in pots and sent out papered separately and packed upright so that the fleshy leaves will not be damaged.

Stonecrops may be propagated either by division, pulling the clumps apart as with aubrietias, or by taking cuttings. The succulent shoots are planted into pans, placing them firmly around the side and into a compost composed of fifty per cent coarse sand or grit and the same proportion of loam. They should be shielded from strong sunlight and kept on the dry side until rooting has taken place. The best time to lift and divide both the sedums and semper-

The cobwebbed house leek

vivums is either in spring or late in autumn, but autumn planting should only be done where the soil is dry and well drained. Most gardeners know only of *Sedum acre* which grows in walls and in sandy places, the variegated form having its bright green shoots tipped with gold, and which is most colourful during the dull days of winter. There are others even more beautiful and which should be in every garden where conditions suit them. The sempervivum could well take the place of cacti for indoor decoration and for collectors they are of easy culture. Though possibly not so grotesque in appearance they are more colourful, whilst they may be used about the garden in so many ways.

Sedums

Species and Varieties

S. ACRE MINOR   This is a tiny form of the 'Golden Wall Pepper'. It forms prostrate mats of rich bronze with tiny yellow flowers.

S. ALBUM-MURALE   It grows 3in tall, has striking mahogany leaves and bears deep pink flowers.

S. ANACAMPSEROS   It has attractive glaucous foliage and bears crimson-purple flowers on 4in stems.

S. ANGLICUM   Native to Britain, it is a carpeter with blue-grey leaves above which are borne loose sprays of pure white flowers.

S. ANOPETALUM GLAUCUM   It forms a silvery grey hummock and bears tiny bright golden flowers.

S. BREVIFOLIUM   A most charming plant, having mealy white leaves tinted with red and studded with large white star-like flowers.

S. CAUTICOLUM   Blooms during September and October with clusters of cherry-red flowers being borne above grey-green foliage.

S. DASYPHYLLUM   It forms a cushion of grey tinged with pink and bears loose sprays of shell-pink flowers during July and August.

S. DOUGLASSII   Taller growing than most, with erect stems of green leaves which turn scarlet and from which are borne stemless yellow flowers.

S. ELLACOMBIANUM   It forms interesting arched stems of toothed leaves and bears flat heads of yellow flowers.

S. EWERSII   Of trailing habit, it has blue-grey leaves and bears flowers of vivid pink.

S. GYPSICOLUM   Forms prostrate mats of purple-green above which it bears glistening white flowers on 2in stems.

S. HISPANICUM   To be found growing across Southern Europe, it has minute spike leaves of grey-green shading to pink and bears flat heads of blush white. The form *minus* has pretty golden foliage.

S. KAMTSCHATICUM VARIEGATUM   Has bronze and cream foliage, and from June until October its orange-yellow flowers are produced on 6in stems.

S. LYDIUM   It forms a tight green clump which turns brilliant crimson in a dry soil. The pinkish-white flowers are borne in August.

S. NEVII   Its rosettes take on autumnal tints, whilst its white flowers, borne in summer, have attractive purple anthers.

S. OREGANUM   The fleshy green foliage turns brilliant crimson, whilst it bears flat heads of golden-orange.

S. APLMERI   A native of Mexico, it forms fleshy grey rosettes and bears sprays of bright orange flowers during May.

S. REFLEXUM CRISTATUM   This is the 'Cockscomb' Sedum, the green leaves being borne along the edges of the fascinating stem. More interesting than beautiful.

S. RHODIOLA   Tight pink rosettes open to a glaucous-green colour whilst it bears heads of lemon-yellow.

S. SEXANGULARE   Its bright green leaves take on a rusty appearance in winter whilst it bears flowers of brilliant gold.

S. SIEBOLDII   A Japanese species, the grey leaves being margined with brown, whilst its flat heads of bright pink flowers are borne during autumn.

S. SPATHULIFOLIUM   A native of North America, it forms rosettes of powdery grey leaves and bears bright yellow star-like blooms on 3in stems. The form *purpureum* has purple-tinted foliage whilst '*Capablanca*' forms tiny silver rosettes.

S. SPURIUM   From the Caucasus, it forms a mat of brilliant crimson and bears a profusion of pale pink flowers early in autumn. The form '*Schorbusoerblut*' has bronzy foliage and bears deep crimson flowers.

S. STRIBNRYI   Very much like *S. acre* but has darker green leaves whilst the flowers are vivid yellow.

S. TERNATUM   Should be in every collection of stonecrops, for it bears its lovely creamy-white flowers with striking black anthers in spring, the only sedum to bloom at that time. Has oval dark green leaves.

S. WATSONI   It has rounded, fleshy, bright green leaves edged with crimson, and through the latter weeks of summer bears large pure white flowers.

Sempervivums

Species and Hybrids

S. ALBERNELLII   A hybrid bearing medium-sized rosettes of bright green.

S. ALLIONII   Its rosettes are small and incurving, and of a brilliant green colour. It bears greenish-white flowers in July.

S. ALPHA   A hybrid, the green hairy rosettes being flushed with crimson.

S. ARACHNOIDEUM   This is the Cobwebbed house leek and a beautiful plant, its succulent leaves being covered with silk-like threads which stretch from tip to tip. The form *stansfieldsii* is even lovelier, for the rosettes are deep crimson, enhanced by the silk threads.

S. ARENARIUM   The rosettes are small and star-like and are of brilliant green, backed with crimson.

S. CANTABRICUM   It forms a large rosette of various shades of green, tipped with bronze, and bears deep pink flowers.

S. CILIOSUM   The small almost ball-like rosettes of grey-green have an attractive netted appearance and bear large golden-yellow flowers.

S. ERYTHRAEUM   It bears flat open rosettes of greyish-mauve which are covered with hairs.

S. FUNCKII   A hybrid having tight bottle-green rosettes, edged with down-like threads of silver.

S. GAMMA   This is a hybrid forming large purple-red rosettes strikingly tipped with green.

S. GLORIOSUM   Most striking in that its large rosettes are of a brilliant crimson colour.

S. GRANDIFLORUM   It forms wide rough green rosettes covered in down and bears large pale yellow flowers.

S. HAGGERI   The crimson rosettes are heavily cobwebbed.

S. HIRSUTUM   The rosettes are covered with downy hairs and are brilliant green, tipped with crimson.

S. JUBILEE   The water-lily rosettes are hairy and of deep green edged maroon.

S. KOSANINII   From Macedonia, it forms large flat rosettes of deep green with purple tips and enhanced by a thick down. The purple flowers have white margins.

S. LEUCANTHUM   The medium-sized rosettes are of a delicate shade of green and are covered with down. The leaves are tipped with purple-bronze.

S. MONTANUM   From the Pyrenees, it forms medium-sized rosettes covered with hairs and which are dark green in colour. The form *stiriacum* has striking brown leaf tips.

S. NEVADENSE   To be found about the Iberian Peninsula, the vivid green rosettes are flat and are as if painted with scarlet. There is also a hairy form, *hirtellum*.

S. ORNATUM   The large rosettes are rich crimson-purple.

S. PITTONI   It forms small, downy incurving rosettes tipped with purple and bears hairy, pale yellow flowers.

S. POWELLII   The rosettes are small and incurved and are of pale green shaded with crimson and pink.

S. PUMILIUM   Forms attractive tiny grey-green rosettes of incurved formation.

S. RUPICOLUM   The large rosettes are thick and fleshy and are of a unique dull purple-brown colour.

S. SCHLEHANII   Its petals are tipped white and all except the tips splashed with brilliant crimson.

S. SEROTINUM   The leaves are extremely thick and fleshy and are of velvety green shaded with brown.

S. SOBOLIFERUM   This is the 'Hen and Chicken' house leek which forms tiny rounded pale green rosettes, and from the leaf joints fall tiny rosettes which take root on contact with the soil.

s. TECTORUM It forms large rosettes of fleshy pointed leaves which are of brilliant green, tipped red. This is the genuine house leek of which there are several forms. 'Nigrum' is most striking, for the leaves are almost black, whilst 'Mrs Guiseppii' bears compact rosettes with bright red tips. The form 'Triste' had chocolate-brown rosettes.

s. VIOLACEUM A hybrid of great beauty, the rosettes, shaped like water lilies, being of a violet-blue colour.

Pompone Chrysanthemums

'This little favourite has tended in no small degree to resuscitate the cultivation of the chrysanthemum.'

MRS BEETON

Held sacred in the gardens of China and Japan since earliest times, these delightful plants did not reach Britain until 1846 when Robert Fortune introduced the 'Chusan Daisy' or *Chrysanthemum rubellum* as it came to be called. Able to withstand intense cold, the plant grows only 20in tall and does not require staking except where the garden is exposed to strong winds. In early autumn, it bears sprays of small circular double blooms resembling the pompoms on the caps of French sailors. Within a few years it came to be planted in every small garden in Britain and in France for it bloomed when most border plants were past their best and the flowers were long lasting when cut and in water. Careful hybridising saw its gradual development and within twenty years its popularity had far exceeded that of the larger flowering chrysanthemum. This plant soon became popular with the florists for the symmetry of the tiny flowers had a particular appeal whilst it was very suited to pot culture.

A number of the early pompones and anemone-flowered varieties are still to be found. One of the finest pompones was 'Model of Perfection', illustrated in *Hardy Florist's Flowers* in which is also mentioned 'Bob', brownish-red and 'Mlle Marthe', white, as being amongst the best pompones. These varieties were also listed by Walter P. Wright in *Popular Garden Flowers* published thirty years later and they are still obtainable after almost a century. 'Bob', also known as 'Little Bob' for it grew no more than 12in tall, was included in the catalogue of John Forbes Ltd, of Hawick, Scotland, as recently as 1960 and as with so many of the old florist's flowers, it is in Scotland that many of the pompones survive.

Culture

The pompones are admirable plants for the small garden for almost all grow less than 2ft tall and are completely hardy. They may be planted with the polyanthus which blooms in spring, the pompones coming into bloom in August and remaining colourful until the year end. Or plant them to the front of a border to extend the display into winter. They require a rich, deeply dug soil which is well supplied with humus to retain summer moisture.

During winter, dig in some decayed manure or used hops and some peat or leaf mould, incorporating it to a depth of 18in.

Young plants should be obtained towards the end of April and planted 20in apart, either in beds or in the border. Where growing in the border, set them near those plants which bloom early and which will give spring protection. These plants will have finished blooming and will have begun to die back before the chrysanthemums make their bushy growth. Firm planting is essential and, as the plants will be small when set out, mark their position with a stick. It is essential that the young plants do not suffer from lack of moisture during their early days in the open ground, and during July and August weekly applications of manure water will enhance the size and colour of the blooms.

After flowering, give a mulch of peat or decayed manure, which is placed around the roots, but not over them; by November next year's flowering shoots will have appeared, a second batch following in May when the soil begins to warm.

For two or three years the plants may remain undisturbed, after which time they should be lifted and divided in the usual way by using two forks. The old woody centre should be discarded. The plants may be lifted early in November each year, or in alternate years, when propagation may be carried out in several ways. Those who do not possess a greenhouse, and when it is not desired to propagate on a commercial scale, may remove the green shoots

A selection of hardy pompone chrysanthemums

with a portion of root attached. These are planted 4in apart in a frame, over which is placed a glass light or a piece of Windolite. There the young plants remain throughout winter, and will be ready for planting out again in April. The plants should be given almost no water during winter and, to prevent mildew, should be treated once a month with flowers of sulphur. Just before the plants are set out they should have the growing point removed to encourage them to build up a bushy plant. Chrysanthemums may also be propagated by division.

This method was recommended by Mr Nevin, who in *The Irish Farmer's and Gardener's Magazine* of 1832 said, 'Any time from the end of April to early July, I detach the young shoots from the old crowns. These are generally furnished with a few small fibres and at this season are about 12in or so in length. With a dibber I then proceed to plant as I would cabbages, into any warm border, allowing 2ft between the plants and 18in in the rows, having previously pinched out the top of each plant. Then give one or two good waterings'. They are amongst the easiest of plants to propagate and grow well.

Varieties

CLARA CURTIS   The flowers are borne in profusion and are of deep strawberry pink.

DUCHESS OF EDINBURGH   Large, globular flowers of deep fiery red.

ELMIRANDA   Early and free flowering, the blooms are a pastel shade of lavender-mauve.

J. B. DUBOIS   In bloom early August, the flowers are of a most attractive shade of soft shell-pink.

MADAME LEFORT   A very old variety growing 2ft tall and bearing flowers of rich orange-bronze.

MARY STOKER   The blooms are small and dainty and of a lovely shade of lemon-yellow.

MIGNON   Early and free flowering, the blooms being of brightest yellow.

PAUL BOISSIER   A French introduction bearing large poms of deep orange-bronze.

PIERCEY'S SEEDLING   Early to bloom, it bears flowers of rich golden-bronze, deepening to terra cotta with age.

PURPLE GEM   The large flowers are of deep rosy-purple, lovely under artificial light.

ST CROUTS   Like so many of the poms, it originated in France and is a charming variety, growing only 16in tall and bearing tiny poms of softest pink.

TOREADOR   The best of its colour, the flowers being of pale moonlight yellow.

WHITE BOUQUET   The best white, the large poms being shaded at the centre with green.

Old-fashioned
Border Plants

'And the Glory of the Garden it shall never pass away'

RUDYARD KIPLING

Many of the old border favourites of cottage gardens, the hardy perennials, are now becoming difficult to find and will become more so as specialist growers turn to roses and flowering shrubs which allow for methods of mass production in their propagation and to make the best possible use of manual labour. Yet from various parts of Britain, especially Scotland and Northern Ireland where the old-fashioned flowers have persisted more so than in England, many of the plants may still be obtained and in a short time a stock may be worked up from only a small beginning.

Bachelor's Buttons

Though an obnoxious weed in the garden, several forms of the buttercup are amongst the most delightful of plants and for centuries have occupied a place in the cottage garden. The meadow crowfoot, so called because the leaves are shaped like a crow's foot, is a taller growing relation of the common buttercup, surprisingly not given its name buttercup until the latter part of the eighteenth century. Before then, they were known as king cups, as Gerard tells us: 'the Crowfoot is called in English, King Kob (cup)' and he continues, 'many do tie a little of the herb, stamped with salt unto any of the fingers against pain of the teeth; for it causes greater pain in the finger than in the tooth; by the means whereof the greater pain taketh away the lesser'.

It is the double form which came to be planted in gardens. Gerard tells that it was 'brought forth out of Lancashire into our London gardens by . . . Master Thomas Hesketh who found it growing wild not far from Latham in Lancashire'. In the *Herbal*, he calls it Bachelor's Buttons and the blooms do indeed resemble the highly polished brass buttons worn on soldiers' tunics. The flowers have more right to be called thus than the double daisy which now appears to have taken the description.

The plant grows 2ft tall and early in summer the large buds begin to unfold to fully double blooms of brilliant gold.

Bergamot

Native of the deciduous woodlands of North America, *Monarda didyma* will grow well in most soils and in full sun or semi-shade. The leaves, stems and roots carry a delicious aromatic lemon perfume when crushed and are much used in perfumery and in pot-pourris, also to make Oswego Tea by an infusion of the leaves in hot water. Both the leaves and the flowers may also be eaten in salads. *M. didyma* bears its red, pink or purple flowers in whorls in candelabra fashion, on 3ft stems and is in bloom from early July until mid-September. It may easily be raised from seed sown in boxes in prepared compost under glass, a cold frame being most suitable whilst the named varieties are increased by root division. The genus is named in honour of Dr Nicholas Monardes of Seville who published his *Herbal* in 1569, but the plant obtained the name Bergamot because of the likeness of its perfume to the Bergamot orange. The plant, which was first mentioned by Parkinson in his *Paradisus*, likes a cool, moist soil.

Species and Varieties

There are a number of excellent varieties of *Monarda didyma*, all of which grow 3ft tall, every part of the plant being aromatic.

ADAM   The blooms, borne in whorls, are of an attractive shade of cerise.

BLUE STOCKING   Of recent introduction, the large refined blooms are of deep violet colouring, the nearest to a 'blue' bargamot.

CAMBRIDGE SCARLET   For long, one of the most striking of all border plants for the flowers are of richest crimson-red.

MELISSA   It has superseded 'Croftway Pink' and bears flowers of clear shell-pink.

PRAIRIE GLOW   A new colour amongst bergamots, the blooms being salmon-pink.

SNOW MAIDEN   It should be planted as a contrast to 'Cambridge Scarlet' for its flowers are of icy-white.

Bleeding Heart

Dicentra spectabilis has been a favourite of the cottage garden for more than a century, and has more country names than any other plant. It was not introduced until 1846 when Robert Fortune found it on the Isle of Chusan. Within a few years it was to be found in almost every cottage garden bearing its drooping heart-shaped flowers from early May until the end of July. From the shape of its flower, it was also known as Ladies' Locket.

The plant enjoys a cool, leafy soil and partial shade. It also likes the company of other plants and once established should never be disturbed. It is not completely hardy but ashes heaped about its crown in autumn should provide it with all the protection it requires and even in an exposed garden it will rarely perish.

A hybrid, 'Bountiful', with its glaucous blue-grey foliage and elegant spikes of rosy-pink lockets is one of the longest flowering of all plants, in bloom from May until September.

Christmas Rose

Helleborus niger is one of the oldest of cultivated plants and is said to have been used by Melampus about the year 1500 BC, to cure the daughters of Proetus, king of Argos, of a mental disease. It is the Black Hellebore, *N. niger*, possibly introduced in Roman times and so called from the black colour of its roots. Gerard said that 'a purgation of hellebor is good for mad and furious men . . . and those molested with melancholy'. At that time the roots were dried and ground to a powder, to be taken like snuff for the relief of headaches and moods of melancholia.

The Christmas rose is perennial and to have bloom the first year 2-year plants should be planted in well-manured ground in March or April, spacing them 18in apart. At all times they should be kept moist and they will appreciate a top dressing of decayed manure given each year in October. For this reason they always bloomed to advantage in the cottage garden. The plants also love some lime rubble in their diet. If one plant, at least, is covered with a cloche in November, not only will the bloom be earlier but will be clean whatever the weather. Earlier bloom may be enjoyed by lifting a root and planting in a large pot (or box) which should be placed in a temperature of 50° F. *H. niger* is like the paeony, a plant of extreme longevity, if regularly top-dressed, and requiring no attention for as long as sixty or more years when each winter it will bear more and more bloom.

Plants appreciate protection from the cold winds of winter and early spring and, as they do not mind partial shade, may be planted at the foot of a wall facing north but where the plants may be sheltered from prevailing winds.

Species and Varieties

HELLEBORUS ATRORUBENS Possibly Parkinson's red-flowered 'Hellebore' which was known to him but which 'perished quickly'. A native of deciduous woodlands of Europe, it bears crimson-purple flowers on 18in stems. The lower leaves are divided into 5 to 9 lobes whilst the upper ones are palmate. A slow grower, it blooms during January and February and is still obtainable from several plantsmen.

H. CORSICUS Native of the island of Corsica, it has bright green foliage and sends up its flowers on stems 3ft tall. The leaves have spiny edges like those of the holly whilst the bright green flowers are borne in bunches of a dozen or more and are a most striking feature of the cottage garden in February.

H. NIGER The earliest into bloom is *H. niger maximus* which grows 2ft tall and bears white flowers, tinted with pink which measure 4in across. The flowers, which resemble those of the hypericum when open, are like small tulips when in bud. The leaves are palmately lobed and are of darkest green. Equally fine is the variety 'Potter's Wheel', bearing enormous pure white flowers, whilst *angustifolius* with its narrow leaves of apple green and flowers of purest white does not bloom until early March.

H. ORIENTALIS   This is the Lenten rose, native of Syria and Asia Minor and a familiar member of cottage gardens since Tudor times. It blooms during March and April, during Lent when it bears large rosy-purple flowers on 20in stems. The leaves are downy and divided into 7- to 9-toothed segments whilst the flowers are borne 2 to 6 to a stem. Crossing with other species has given rise to hybrid varieties of various shades of pink, purple and red.

Cross of Jerusalem

Also called the Scarlet Campion, *Lychnis chalcedonica* is believed to have been introduced into Europe during the time of the Crusades for in all European countries it has the same name, Cross of Jerusalem, from the cross formed by the petals of the tiny flowers, many of which go to make up a head of great brilliance.

The plant is native of southern Russia and Turkey from where it reached the Middle East and it is possible it was brought back to Western Europe by those returning from the pilgrimages abroad, since when it has remained amongst the most beloved of all cottage garden plants.

With its dark green leaves and holding its flame-coloured flowers on stems 3 to 4ft long, it stands out in any company, an established plant having few rivals for the amount of colour it will produce compared with the amount of garden space it occupies. It is also of easy culture and has the endurance of the paeony.

Lyte in his *Herbal* (1578) said that the tiny flowers were 'clustered together at the top of the stalks after the manner of Sweet Williams . . . of the colour of red lead', an excellent description, and of the double form which appeared just before the publication of the *Paradisus*, Parkinson wrote of 'this glorious flower, as rare as it is beautiful . . .' At the same time appeared a double white-flowered variety, considered by the Dutch to be one of the most choice of all flowers.

The plant is in bloom during July and August. It should be planted in November for it is not particular as to soil, neither is it troubled by excess moisture. Propagation is by division, removing the offsets and re-planting about 18in apart and this should be done every 4 or 5 years. To prolong the life of the plant, the stems should be cut down to within 6in of the ground as soon as possible after flowering. This is especially advisable with the double variety.

Day Lily

Though of the lily family, *Hemerocallis flava* is propagated by division of the roots in autumn and spring. The plants require a deeply dug soil and will flourish either in full sun or partial shade. They bloom during July and

August, lasting only for a day but others take their place in one long succession over a period of eight weeks. The funnel-shaped flowers are borne in clusters on 2 to 3ft stems above a clump of grass-like leaves. Those of yellow colour usually carry the sweet perfume of the sweetly scented *H. flava*, a native of Central Europe which is to be found growing in pastureland, scenting the air for a distance when warmed by the summer sunshine. Many strikingly lovely hybrids have been raised during the past decade varying in colour from blackish red to orchid pink, all of them descended from *H. flava* and *H. fulva*, the latter a scentless species bearing orange flowers. They were to be found growing in Gerard's garden and may have been familiar to Shakespeare. They were then known as Asphodel Lilies for they have roots like those of the Asphodel and bear a flower of lily form.

Varieties

APOLLO   The flowers are large and of rich apricot-orange with a cream edge.
GOLDEN SCEPTRE   It grows 3ft tall and bears large clusters of bloom of a unique shade of bright Empire yellow.
GOLDEN WEST   Taller growing than most, reaching a height of 3½ft and bears large flowers of deep golden-yellow.
HONEYSUCKLE   Like all the yellows it is tall growing, the deep golden-yellow blooms having a rich honeysuckle perfume.
HYPERION   It grows 2ft tall and bears large blooms of pale citron-yellow with a delicious sweet perfume.
IRIS, LADY LAWRENCE   It grows only 18in tall and bears large flowers of creamy-apricot which are sweetly scented.
JAS. KELSEY   It bears sparkling clusters of medium-sized flowers of soft buttery yellow.
MARY RANDALL   It grows 30in tall and bears flowers of a soft lemon-yellow with a deeper yellow line down each petal.
PINK CHARM   Late flowering, it is well named for the small, dainty blooms are of a lovely shade of old-rose, tinted with buff.
PINK DAMASK   The large handsome blooms are of soft rose-pink, like old Damask silk.
RADIANT   Received an Award of Merit for its bright golden-apricot flowers which possess exceptional perfume and are borne in profusion.

Double Daisy

Useful for spring bedding, to plant with violettas or primroses in nooks about the rock garden, *Bellis perennis*, the double daisy, has probably been held in greater esteem by poets and nobility than any other flower.

Chaucer wrote in *The Legend of Good Women*:

> Of all the flowers in the meade
> Then love I most those floures white and redde,
> Such that men call daisies in our town . . .
> When it upriseth early by the morrow,
> That blissful sight softeneth all my sorrow.

Again, he alludes to its Anglo-Saxon name of 'daeyeseage', meaning 'the eye of the day', for it is the first flower to open each morning and from this it takes its name. The French know it as Pâquerette because it is usually in fullness of bloom at the approach of Pâques (Easter), but its botanical name comes from the Latin *bellus*, 'pretty'.

The pink double daisy is beautifully shown in a water colour of about 1570 attributed to Jaques le Moyne, several of whose paintings have survived and are to be seen in London's Victoria and Albert Museum. They are amongst the most botanically skilled of all flower paintings and most of them are enhanced by butterflies and moths most accurately depicted.

Several varieties of the double daisy dating from the early days of the nineteenth century survive, one of the loveliest being 'Dresden China', with its tiny blooms, tightly packed with multitudes of quilled petals of a glorious shade of shell-pink. It is one of the most beautiful of all small plants. And of similar age is the scarlet 'Rob Roy' which appeared shortly after the appearance of Scott's novel in 1818. The little scarlet buttons are borne on 3in stems and 'The Pearl', bearing equally small blooms of pearly white, acts as a pleasing contrast.

Nor should *Bellis prolifera*, the 'Hen and Chickens' of old cottage gardens, be forgotten. Tiny flowerets develop from the main bloom and dangle around the plant like chickens around the mother hen. It is a delightful plant for a small pot in a sunny window. This and the named varieties of the double daisy require a soil which contains some humus for they are intolerant of dry conditions in summer. It is completely hardy anywhere but to be long living it requires frequent division and enjoys best a position of semi-shade. Prepare the soil as for pansies and primroses when they will prove perennial.

Fair Maids of France

Ranunculus aconitifolius is believed to have reached England with the Huguenots fleeing from the Massacre of St Bartholomew in 1572 for the plants grow wild in parts of France. It is a delightful plant and came to be widely grown in cottage gardens but has almost disappeared, probably because it is difficult to establish. It grows 2 to 3ft tall and bears in June, on branching stems, multitudes of pure white buttons, double, like tiny pompone chrysanthemums, hence it was one of many flowers to be called Bachelor's Buttons. Gerard told us that it 'grew in the gardens of lovers of strange and beautiful plants', denoting its rarity at the time the *Herbal* was published in

Double daisies

1596. The whiteness of the flowers is enhanced by the dark green leaves, attractively lobed like those of other flowering plants of the family. The plant came to be called Fair Maids of Kent but the origin of the name is unknown to the author.

Like most members of the *Ranunculus* family, it should be planted in April so that the tuberous roots do not decay through excessive winter moisture whilst still dormant. Plant 12in apart with the roots on a layer of sand or peat.

Globe Flower

Trollius europeus is native to the British Isles and was introduced to country gardens at an early date. Clusius has said that he saw it in London gardens about 1580 and it has remained, like the Christmas rose, virtually unchanged since its cultivation as a garden plant. *T. asiaticus*, the Orange Globe-flower of north China, is similar in every way except that its flowers are more orange in colour. It was introduced early in the eighteenth century and has since given rise to a number of varieties such as 'Salamander', fiery orange; 'Goldquelle', golden-yellow; and 'Canary Bird', canary-yellow.

They grow 2 to 3ft in height and enjoy a damp soil and partial shade when the flowers will be long lasting. Propagation is by division of the roots in autumn, re-planting them 18in apart.

Jacob's Ladder

Flourishing in full sun and partial shade and tolerant of all soil conditions, *Polymonium coeruleum* is a splendid plant for the garden, coming into bloom in May and covering itself with flowers of brilliant blue. The variety 'Blue Pearl' grows about 12in tall and 'Sapphire' about 18in. Both are lovely and will bloom from May until the end of July. It is a native plant well loved by the first Elizabethan gardeners and has been grown in cottage gardens since earliest times under the name of the Blue or Greek Valerian.

Lady's Smock

Cardamine pratensis is to be found in damp places, by the side of streams and in low-lying meadowland. A delightful native plant, it blooms at Lady-tide and so was dedicated to our Lady. It is also known as Cuckoo-flower for it blooms in May and June when the cuckoo arrives and its pleasing call echoes across the countryside.

Isaac Walton wrote: 'looking down in the meadow, (I) could see there a boy gathering lilies and lady's smocks . . . to make garlands suitable to this present month of May'.

Seen from a distance, the flowers resemble the smocks or chemises laid out by maidens of Elizabethan times, to dry and bleach in the sun. It was always

Ranunculus from a coloured engraving of 1837: (*top left*) 'Adolphus';
(*top right*) 'Victoria'; (*bottom left*) 'Diadem'; (*bottom right*) 'Governor'

in demand by countrymen for its leaves were used in salads and have the bitter taste and the same health-giving qualities as watercress, being of the same family.

It was the double form *C. pratensis flore plena* that was for long a familiar sight in cottage gardens but is now rarely seen. The flowers have the metallic appearance of polished silver and growing 12in tall, Henry Phillips in the *Flora Historica* says 'should be in every garden where the soil tends to be damp'.

Leopard's-bane

Doronicum plantagineum is a native of Central Europe where its poisonous roots were dried and mixed with meat to rid the countryside of unwanted animals, hence its ancient name of Leopard's-bane. There is a story that the famous botanist Conrad Gesner killed himself by taking 2 drams of the root as an experiment and Matthiolus, after whom the scented stock is named, gave it to a dog which died immediately. Yet it is a much appreciated plant for it blooms early in the year, during April and May when few other border plants are in bloom and, enjoying partial shade, will brighten the darkest corner with its golden flowers for which purpose it was to be found in every cottage garden.

Gerard tells that it grew in his garden in London and also mentions that a friend of his found it growing wild in the hilly regions of Northumberland. However, it may at some time have become naturalised, having possibly been introduced by the Romans for the poisoning of wild animals.

It is a plant of extreme hardiness which will flourish in all soils. It has stalked heart-shaped leaves and is covered in glandular hairs. On the end of 3ft stems, solitary flowers are borne and which have rayed petals of deep golden-yellow. A variety named after Rev Harpur Crewe is the best form whilst 'Spring Beauty' is a most outstanding introduction, bearing fully double blooms of deepest yellow on 12in stems.

London Pride

Saxifraga umbrosa is a plant that has been grown since earliest times for its properties of 'breaking up stone' in the bladder which is the meaning of its name. It is a native plant, to be found about the mountains of Donegal and Mayo and of the craggy hills of North Yorkshire and was in almost every cottage garden in that part of the country where its name was None-So-Pretty. Indeed, few flowers have been more attractively served by nature for the tiny petals are pointed with a delicacy seen in few other flowers and which may be fully appreciated only through a microscope. The flowers are borne in sprays which arise on 12in stems from a rosette of dark green glossy leaves and, because of its neat habit, it was widely used for an edging to small garden beds and borders. It is a plant of extreme hardiness and also flourishes under town garden conditions so that by Parkinson's time it had become widely planted in London gardens, hence its name London Pride. Miss Alice Coats, however, in *Flowers and their Histories*, believes the plant received its name from Mr George London, Royal Gardener to William III in 1688, who made liberal use of it in the Royal gardens of Hampton Court and Kensington Palace. It grows well in shade and will rapidly propagate itself by offsets. Native of the rocky limestone formations, it enjoys a soil containing limestone chippings and also grows well in a rockery constructed of limestone.

Moon Daisy

One of the loveliest flowers of our pastures, the ox-eye or dog daisy, has been grown in cottage gardens since earliest times. It is *Chrysanthemum leucanthemum* and came to be called the marguerite when Margaret of Anjou, queen of Henry VI, at the age of 15, took the flower as her emblem in 1445, perhaps as a reminder of the alpine meadows of Anjou where it also flourishes. But it was the moon daisy of the Pyrenees, *C. maximum*, which came to be so much planted for it flourished in all soils and in the coldest of gardens, bearing its large snow-white single flowers from July until October. *C. maximum* reached Britain early in the nineteenth century and quickly superseded the old marguerite for it was more robust in every way. Autumn is the most suitable time for its planting, dividing the roots into offsets and planting them 15in apart. They will quickly grow into large clumps each capable of bearing, on 3–4ft stems, fifty or more flowers in a single summer.

Varieties

COBHAM GOLD   It was found by Lord Darnley in the gardens of Cobham Hall and bears large fully double blooms with a definite flush of gold.

DROITWICH BEAUTY   It grows 3ft tall and bears enormous blooms of purest white with frilly petals.

ESTHER READ   Growing less than 20in tall, it has been more widely planted than any cut flower, so much so that of recent years, the plant has lost vigour. The pure white flowers are extremely double and are borne with freedom all through summer.

FIONA COGHILL   It is similar to 'Esther Read' in all respects and being new the plants are vigorous and free flowering.

HORACE READ   Will attain a height of 4ft and bears large double white flowers of the quality of 'Blanche Poitou' chrysanthemum.

H. SEIBERT   The single flowers are as large as a dinner plate and open flat with beautifully cut petals.

MOONLIGHT   Similar to 'Cobham Gold' except that the yellow flush is more pronounced and does not fade with age.

Chrysanthemum maximum, a modern version of the old marguerite

THOMAS KILLIN A most unusual form, bearing large pure white flowers with an attractive 'anemone' centre, comprising multitudes of tiny petals.

WIRRAL SNOWBALL Growing only 2ft tall it is suitable for the front of a border. The blooms are almost the size of a Japanese chrysanthemum, like enormous white globes.

Paeony

Named by the ancient Greeks after Paeon, who used the milk-like extract from the roots to cure the wounded Pluto. To the Greeks, and the peoples of those countries of the Eastern Mediterranean, the plant was held in something of awe for the seeds of certain species tend to give off a glow at night. This is due to a phosphorescent quality, and it was believed that both the seeds and the roots should be obtained only during the dead of night. At that time the roots were used for healing wounds, whilst the seeds were infused in rain water to make a special 'tea'. It was also believed that they would act as a charm against evil if carried in the pocket.

A paeony believed to be native to Britain, *P. mascula*, may well have been introduced from Europe by the early Christians, for the few places where the plants are now still to be found growing wild are situated close to the sites of ancient monasteries. The beautiful single flowers are more than 4in in diameter, the stamens being tipped with gold. The blooms are enhanced by the glossy, dark green foliage of the plant, whilst the seed vessels are most attractive during autumn when they open to reveal rose-red seeds which have the appearance of coral. For this reason the plant is also known as *P. corallina*.

Whereas *P. mascula* is known as the male paeony, *P. feminea* or *P. officinalis* was known as the female paeony. This was the plant so well known to the Greeks, but it was the double form of *P. officinalis* that was to become familiar in our gardens. It was from the Mediterranean regions that the first plants of the double paeony reached Britain some time before the beginning of the sixteenth century, but exactly when is not known, though it is believed that *P. officinalis* was cultivated during Saxon times.

The crimson-flowered herbaceous paeony, *P. officinalis* (and its pink counterpart), is to be so often found in the gardens of ancient manor house and country cottage because of the great durability of the plant. It has been described as being as hardy and as durable as the dock which is true, for when once established, the plants will make dense bushes growing thicker than they grow tall and will bear as many as two dozen blooms per plant year after year.

They resent disturbance and should be planted only where they will be fully permanent, in the same way as one plants a tree or a hedge. Even a single plant in a small border will produce a magnificent display each year and at a time when the border will generally be lacking in colour. It is only during about ten weeks of the year that the paeony is quite dormant, from the middle of September until early December and if at all possible planting should be done at this time. By planting in October after the foliage has died back, the roots will become established before the severe weather and will get away to a good start as soon as the ground begins to warm in spring.

The actual planting of the roots is extremely important. Paeony roots are thick and fleshy, being woody and tuberous-like, and quite apart from the need to guard against breakage of the crown buds, is the need to handle the roots with care for they are easily broken. A two-year-old root containing two to three buds or eyes will be most suitable, for it will be vigorous and will grow away rapidly, whereas an old root will take considerably longer to establish.

Of the many lovely varieties of herbaceous paeony, 'Alice Harding' with its incurved blooms of creamy-white and 'Albatross', its huge white blooms being tipped with crimson, are outstanding. 'Claire Dubois' bears large blooms of satin-pink edged with silver whilst 'Gayborder June' bears flowers of carmine-red. 'Kelway's Queen' bears flowers of shrimp-pink, likewise 'Marie Crousse'. Magnificent is 'Phillipe Rivoire', its crimson blooms having a black sheen and the perfume of the 'tea' rose.

Pentstemon

One of the few plants of the New World taken up by florists for the handsome dangling tubular bells are circular at the mouth, the petals being slightly rolled back in a most attractive manner. *P. hartwegi*, discovered by Professor Humboldt in Mexico, growing at an elevation of more than 10,000ft and introduced in 1828, is the chief parent of the florist's varieties. Several other species were discovered in north-west America by David Douglas, the explorer who met with a cruel death early in 1835 when on an expedition to the Sandwich Islands. From *P. hartwegi* and other species, numerous hybrid varieties were introduced from 1835 onwards and came to be widely grown as bedding plants and to beautify the border.

Hardy in the more favourably situated gardens, especially in the western parts of the British Isles where they may be permanent plants of the garden, they were especially cultivated by the Scottish growers who have maintained extensive collections up to the present time. In the colder parts, it is usual to lift the plants in November, to winter them under glass and to plant out again in May.

Cuttings, which form at the base of the plant, are removed early in September and planted in boxes, pots or frames containing a sandy compost. Plant 2in apart and place in a frame or greenhouse, shading them from strong sunlight when they will root in about four weeks. The plants should not be disturbed until March when they are moved to small pots and grown-on for 6–8 weeks in a frame or beneath barn cloches. They will have formed sturdy plants to be set out towards the end of spring.

The pentstemon requires a well drained sandy soil containing some decayed manure and peat or leaf mould. In a heavy, badly drained soil the plants may perish during winter. But this is an easily grown plant which blooms from July until November when, apart from chrysanthemums and Michaelmas daisies, there is little other colour in the garden. At this time, no plant can match the pentstemon for brightness.

At least fifty varieties are obtainable, many dating from the mid-nineteenth century. They are obtainable in shades of pink, rose, purple, scarlet and crimson and intermediate shades. Amongst the finest are 'Countess of Haddington', bearing large trumpets of rich crimson, veined with purple, and 'Countess of Dalkeith', the deep purple bells having a pure white throat. 'Lady Sherborne' is of unusual colouring, bearing trumpets of shell pink margined with chocolate-brown around the edge, whilst 'Mrs J. Purser' bears rose-pink flowers pencilled with darker rose. Two of the finest scarlet varieties are 'Thomas H. Cook' and 'Chester Scarlet', both of which bear large stately spikes of the most intense red. Also attractive is 'Roderick Mackenzie' with its large bells of richest purple and 'Lady Monckton', pale lilac with a white throat. Delightful, too, is 'Lady Lloyd' which forms a handsome spike of creamy-white bells margined with rosy-pink.

Rock Cress

One of the most beautiful and valuable plants of the garden, the purple rock-cress, was given its name, *aubrietia*, in honour of the French botanist Monsieur Aubriet. It is to be found growing naturally in Greece and Asia Minor, about the lower rock formations where its trailing habit and great freedom of flowering produces a most striking effect against the boulders. It was introduced to Britain in 1710 and quickly adapted itself to the climate. Tolerant of intense cold it does not appreciate an excess of moisture about its roots, for which reason it is happiest where growing on a wall or rockery where winter moisture may readily drain away. No garden plant bears a more richly coloured bloom, nor one of such clear colouring. Whilst bearing the greater part of its bloom during May and early June, it is valuable in bridging the gap between the late spring and early summer flowering plants.

The many-named varieties of the modern aubrietia are hybrids descended from several species to be found in Southern Europe. Of these, *A. leichtlinii* forms a thick carpet of rose-coloured blooms; *A. hendersonii* bears a bloom of reddish-purple colour; whilst *A. olympica* bears lilac-blue flowers. Each of these species has been widely used for hybridising, the result being many hybrid varieties of quite outstanding beauty. Another species, *A. erubescens*, which has also been used in the early hybridising, bears a blush-white bloom, and yet the white-flowered *aubrietia* which would prove such a striking contrast to the vivid crimsons and purples has yet to be raised.

Cultural Requirements

The aubrietia likes an open, sunny position, and in shade will not bloom profusely, making thick mats of foliage but bearing little bloom. Few plants are better able to tolerate a dry soil and a situation fully exposed to the early summer sun as this, and advantage should be taken of its ability to flourish under such conditions. What a wonderful display can be obtained by planting the late-flowering daffodils, such as the white 'Beersheba', against a background of trailing purple-flowered aubrietia, both of which will be in full bloom together. Or the aubrietia may also be used as a background to yellow May-flowering tulips, or, again, use white tulips with crimson aubrietia. And if there is no suitable place over which the aubrietia may trail, then plant the compact varieties in beds, interplanting with either daffodils or tulips. After flowering, the bulbs may be removed without disturbing the aubrietias, their place being taken by summer-flowering plants. Aubrietias should not be moved from the open ground later than the end of March, this month being the only time for transplanting plants from the open ground or from boxes, as they do not like moving in autumn. Like almost all blue-flowering plants, early spring is the most suitable time for planting, though plants from pots may be set out at almost any time, providing the soil is friable. More disappointment is caused in growing aubrietias by planting at the wrong time than almost by any other cause, for of all plants they resent root disturbance. Where established, the plants should be left alone, being kept neat and tidy by

Essex cottage garden with honeysuckle and valerian

the removal of unduly long shoots after flowering or early in autumn.

Aubrietias like a sandy, well-drained soil and one which is not acid. They do, in fact, flourish in a chalky soil, which will generally be hot and dry. When planting in a town garden, where the soil may have been worked for many years, and which will be of an acid nature due to deposits of soot and sulphur, it will be advisable to work in some lime rubble or dress with hydrated lime during winter before planting in early spring. If the soil is in any way heavy, incorporate some shingle and a little decayed manure. Indeed, well-decayed cow manure or old mushroom bed compost will be much appreciated by the plants whatever the condition of the soil.

Plant firmly, but not too deeply, and allow those varieties of vigorous trailing habit at least 18in between each plant, for within two years they will have closed up the spaces. For stock-plant purposes, several plants of as large a number of varieties as possible may be planted on the flat, in slightly raised beds of well-drained soil to prevent the roots decaying during winter. Or the plants may be set 18in apart along a wall where their beauty may be best appreciated. Each plant or group of plants should be carefully named, for there are more than a hundred named varieties, and whilst many show only a slight deviation in colour, in size and form of the bloom many vary considerably.

Propagation

The aubrietia is not one of the easiest plants to propagate, for the cuttings damp off readily. Established plants may be lifted and divided by pulling them to pieces, the most suitable time being in March. Another method is to pull off long shoots containing several inches of stem in early July after flowering, and these may be planted in trenches of sandy soil. Here they will root if kept comfortably moist but in no way saturated. July generally being a month of wet weather, the shoots will be best covered by cloches during heavy rain or they may damp off at soil level. The cloches should be shaded to prevent the cuttings being scorched by the sun when it shines.

The best method of increasing stock, however, is to propagate from sturdy cuttings. These should be removed immediately after flowering, detaching them with about 4in of stem and removing the lower leaves to prevent them damping off when inserted in the compost. Several dozen such cuttings may be removed from a two-year-old plant and this will not only stimulate the plant into new growth but will keep it tidy and free of straggling shoots. The cuttings should be rooted in a frame so that moisture and shade may be regulated. The compost should be made up of moist peat and coarse sand in equal parts. Soil, unless sterilised, should not be used, for it will almost always cause damping off, however carefully the cuttings are watered. Insert the cuttings 3in apart and make them quite firm. If the compost is moist there should be no need to water them in but give a dusting with green flowers of sulphur to guard against mildew, and water only when the compost begins to dry out.

To create a humid atmosphere which will encourage rapid rooting, the frame should be kept closed, the cuttings being shaded by whitening the glass or polythene sheeting may be used. To cover the cuttings will also prevent them being saturated by heavy rains. As soon as rooting commences, which will be in about a month, or a week earlier if the cuttings are dipped into hormone powder before insertion, they should be given a little more moisture and plenty of fresh air, the frame lights being removed entirely excepting during periods of heavy rain.

By the end of August, the rooted cuttings will be ready for potting, for in this way they will be far more satisfactory and may be planted at any time, even when in full bloom, when they will have a most attractive appearance. The potting compost should consist of fibrous loam, decayed manure and coarse sand, in equal parts, and to which is added a sprinkling of super-phosphate of lime to encourage a vigorous root action. After potting, the plants may be replaced in the frame, where they may be protected from continuous rains and unduly severe weather until spring. By then they will have made bushy plants and be ready for planting out in their flowering quarters. Plants from pots may be removed at any time if not allowed to suffer from lack of moisture.

Choice Varieties

BARKER'S DOUBLE   The semi-double blooms are of a deep shade of bright rose-red. It makes a plant of vigorous habit but is not so reliable as the more recently introduced doubles.

BELISHA BEACON   A plant of compact habit which bears dainty flowers of rose-red.

BONFIRE   Makes a neat, compact plant and bears masses of small blooms of glowing crimson. Very late.

BRESSINGHAM CHARM   Of neat, compact habit, it bears large blooms of clear blue.

BRESSINGHAM PINK   The only double pink, the blooms being extremely large and of a lovely shade of clear pink.

CAMBRIA   An old favourite bearing bright red blooms and which also flowers well in autumn.

CARNIVAL   The blooms are large and of a deep purple colour. It makes a plant of trailing habit.

CHURCH KNOWLE   A fine old variety of compact habit, the blooms are of a unique shade of greyish blue.

DR MULES   It makes a compact plant and is one of the most free-flowering of all aubrietias, the blooms being glowing purple.

FIRE KING   In its improved form it is a strong grower and the first aubrietia to bloom, the flowers being rich crimson.

GLORIOSA   A grand old variety, its clear pink blooms being the largest of all.

GODSTONE   The blooms are large and borne in masses and are of a clear shade of deepest violet.

GREENCOURT PURPLE   It is the best of all the purple varieties and the blooms are fully double.

GURGEDYKE   The flowers are large and the deepest purple of all.

JOAN ALLEN   The best crimson for the blooms are large and double whilst it blooms over a long time.

LANCASHIRE BEAUTY   One of the earliest to bloom, bearing large blooms of soft powder-blue.

LISSADELL PINK   Shell-pink blooms have a striking white eye.

LODGE CRAVE   An outstanding variety bearing huge blooms of violet-blue.

MAGICIAN   Of compact habit and very free-flowering, the blooms are of deep pure purple.

MAURICE PRICHARD   Of neat habit, the blooms are a delicate satin-pink.

MRS J. S. BAKER   Free-flowering, the bright violet-mauve blooms have an attractive white eye.

MRS RODEWALD   One of the very best crimson-flowered varieties, for the blooms are large and borne with profusion.

PETER BARR   The earliest of its colour and a beauty, its red and purple blooms being of almost bi-coloured appearance and produced in masses.

PINK SPARK   The blooms are large and of bright clear pink and it is the last variety to bloom. Now difficult to obtain.

PRICHARD'S AI   A fine variety of vigorous, trailing habit, bearing flowers of deep purple-blue with a striking white eye.

RIVERSLEA   A strong grower, bearing large deep pink blooms over a long period.

ROSEA SPLENDENS   Of compact habit and extremely free-flowering, the large blooms are rose-pink.

RUSSELL'S CRIMSON   Of neat habit, the dainty blooms are of rich glowing crimson.

SOUTER'S VIOLET   A magnificent variety, bearing large rounded blooms of richest royal-purple.

STOCK-FLOWERED PINK   So named because its clear pink blooms are semi-double and have the appearance of pink stocks.

STUDLAND   The author's favourite, the large refined blooms being of clearest blue. It makes a plant of compact habit and blooms profusely.

TRIUMPHANT   Almost the only variety of its colour, best described as of clear mid-blue without a trace of mauve.

VIVID   Of compact habit and bearing masses of deep pink flowers.

WANDA   Possibly the best of all aubrietias, the clear bright red blooms are fully double and are produced early and over a long period.

Solomon's Seal

Now rarely seen, *Polygonatum multiflorum* has for centuries been one of the loveliest of cottage garden plants sending up its gracefully arching stems to a height of 2ft and bearing in May and June, drooping bells of cool greenish-white. It is a perennial with dark green glossy leaves borne, like the flowers, all along the stem like a ladder, hence its name ladder-to-heaven. A plant of deciduous woodlands, it loves the shade and beneath it primroses may be planted and will still be in bloom when the Solomon's seal is opening its dainty bells in early summer.

There is a belief that the name 'seal' was given the plant because of the markings of the fleshy stem which when cut transversely, show the impression of the seal of Solomon. More credible is the theory of Dioscorides who said that the roots when dry and crushed and placed on flesh wounds caused them to be healed (sealed) in the quickest possible time, hence Solomon's heal, became Solomon's seal. A medical authority of the reign of Elizabeth I has said that the roots 'stamped whilst fresh and green and applied to the skin, taketh away in one night, any bruise gotten by woman's wilfulness in stumbling upon their nasty husband's fists'. From the bells a toilet water was distilled.

The roots are best planted in November just below the surface of the soil which should contain some humus to help maintain moisture during the summer months.

Spiderwort

Tradescantia virginica, a most interesting plant, was introduced by John Tradescant the Elder who received plants whilst travelling in Europe which had reached Holland from Virginia several years previously. Tradescant was then gardener to Charles I and Queen Henrietta Maria, when Parkinson was the Royal botanist. By the mid-seventeenth century the plant was to be found in every cottager's garden, Sir Thomas Hanmer when describing it in 1659, saying that it had 'deep blew-coloured flowers' but by then the original plant had been joined by others bearing red, pale blue and white flowers.

It received its country name of spiderwort from the belief that the plant was of the same family as the *Phalangium*, the juice of which was used as a cure for the bite of poisonous spiders. It is a member of the *commelina* family and is an excellent plant for a town garden whilst it also grows well in partial shade. It has dark green purple-veined leaves which grow from the stem and throughout the early weeks of summer, bears its attractive three-petalled flowers backed by three long green outer sepals, on 2ft stems. Of extreme hardiness, it is a most interesting plant, bridging the gap between the spring and summer flowering plants, and it needs the minimum of attention, being divided every fourth year or so to maintain its vigour and re-planting into a well-drained loamy soil for, like most blue flowering plants, it is not tolerant of excess moisture during the dormant season.

Amongst the best varieties is 'Osprey', bearing large flowers of purest white, enhanced by the green sepals; *coerulea plena*, sky-blue and double; 'Purple Dome'; and 'Valour', crimson-purple.

Sweet Rocket

Hesperis matronalis (or dame's violet) is the botanical name for the flowers carry the unmistakable scent of the violet, much resembling the perfume of the wallflower, to which it is closely related. Like the stock and wallflower, the scent has undertones of cloves which makes it more pleasing and lasting.

Probably native of the British Isles as well as of Central Europe, it grows 3ft tall with ovate lance-shaped leaves 'of a dark green colour, snipt about the edges', wrote Gerard, 'the flowers come forth at the top of the branches, like those of the Stock gillyflower . . .'. The small white or purple cross-shaped flowers are borne during June and July and in the words of an early nineteenth-century writer 'no flower garden ought to be without them; their neat habit, beauty, and particular fragrance, alike recommend them'.

But it was the double forms in white and purple that endeared the plant to early gardeners. They grew them in pots and in open ground beds, restricting the height by pinching out the leader shoot. The plants then grew only 20in tall and formed dense bushy growth composed of numerous basal shoots which were easily detached and grown-on. Or where the plants were not to be propagated, they produced numerous flowering stems the following year and were a billowing mass of white or purple foam, scenting the air afar.

The plant requires a well-drained sandy soil containing a little decayed manure and some peat or leaf mould. Plant in autumn for it is completely hardy, and space 12in apart.

Sweet William

The first writer to notice this plant was Dr Dodoens who, in 1554 when physician to the Emperor Charles V of Germany, published his *New Herbal*. Gerard, writing some years later speaks of it as 'a common flower' and for the first time refers to it as the Sweet William, saying 'these plants are not used either in mete or medicine but are esteemed for their beauty, to deck up gardens and the bosoms of the beautiful' for which purpose they were used at the French Court early in the nineteenth century.

The flower, which came to be known as the auricula-eyed Sweet William, was taken up by the Paisley weavers along with the pink for its inner circles of purple or crimson had an appeal similar to the lacing of the pinks. That held in most esteem, however, was the double flowering form, known as 'King Willie'. Until the ending of World War II it was to be found in cottage gardens everywhere. It is now rare though it grows in several gardens in Northern Ireland.

It is a handsome flower with several rows of petals and as it does not set seed must be propagated from cuttings or by layering as for carnations. Rooted cuttings should be grown-on in small pots during winter to be planted out in spring, spacing them 9in apart.

It requires a rich well-drained soil but like all *dianthus*, requires lime in its diet, preferably in the form of lime rubble (mortar).

Venus' Navel-wort

Omphalodes verna, native of southern Europe, is a delightful carpeting plant and was introduced during Charles I's reign when it quickly became a favourite of the cottage garden. Though quite happy in partial shade, in full sunlight it makes a superb display, during March and April being a sheet of brilliant blue, hence its name of Bright-eyed Mary, the flowers resembling forget-me-nots both in colour and in form. There is also a white variety, *alba*, which makes a fitting companion to the blue. The plants will form dense mats through which dwarf bulbs may push themselves up creating a delightful picture as soon as the snow has melted and the sun gathers strength. The plant obtained its name Venus' navel-wort from the peculiar dome shape of its seeds.

Wallflower

Those who know only the single red and yellow wallflowers would find it hard to believe to what extent the plant was prized a century ago. In *The Floricultural Cabinet* for December 1848 appeared a short piece on the culture of wallflowers, the writer saying that those 'having double flowers have been cultivated in Britain for three centuries; we have the blood-red, black, golden and pale yellow, and another which is nearly green. They are worthy of every attention and are so highly esteemed in some of the northern counties that they rank as prize (show) flowers and form a class for competition. It is surprising to see the very large specimens which are produced, the spikes in bloom measuring from 18–24in long.'

The plant is a member of the same family with its four cross-shaped petals that includes the stock and sweet rocket which also endeared themselves to early gardeners on account of their delicious scent. They were all known as gillyflowers, like the Sweet William for it had the same clear perfume. To Parkinson, the wallflower was the wall-gillyflower. In the *Paradisus*, he described seven kinds, including the double red and double yellow, saying that 'the sweetness of the flowers causeth them to be used for nosegays and to deck up houses'. So often was the flower used as a nosegay that it was for this reason given its botanical name *Cheiranthus*, meaning 'hand-flower', one held and carried in the hand for its perfume 'cheered' the spirits.

Native of southern Europe, it possibly reached England with the Norman invasion for it was to be found on the walls of castles and abbeys, probably rooted to stone sent over from France for their building.

It was the double flowering wallflowers that interested the florists and as they did not set seed, they were propagated by cuttings. After flowering, the blooms are removed and the plants allowed to remain in the beds. They form an abundance of shoots from the base which are removed when about 3in long. The lower leaves are removed and the cuttings inserted in boxes of sandy compost or around the side of a pot. Shade from the sun and syringe if they wilt. They will root in four weeks when they are moved to small pots and grown-on in a frame until early March, to be planted into their flowering quarters to bloom the following year. In this way there will always be a stock of young plants available.

Double wallflowers grow best in a well-drained sandy soil, containing a little decayed manure and they require an open, sunny situation. During the summer, give the plants ample supplies of moisture to keep them growing.

Two of the oldest varieties are still occasionally to be found but the ease with which the single wallflower is raised from seed has, in this age of mass production, meant that the doubles which require vegetative propagation, have become more difficult to find. Parkinson's old double red, known as the 'Bloody Warrior', is almost extinct but the old double yellow, rediscovered in a Shropshire garden early in the century by Rev Harpur Crewe, Rector of Drayton Beauchamp, is still obtainable and bears his name.

Bibliography

Book of Flowers, The	Maria Merian
Catalogue of Pinks (1822)	Thomas Hogg
Complete Florilege, The (1665)	John Rea
Cottage Gardener, The (1849)	George Johnson
Country Housewife's Garden, The (1618)	William Lawson
English Flower Garden, The (1883)	William Robinson
Every Man His Own Gardener (1767)	Mawe and Abercrombie
Flora Historica (1824)	Henry Phillips
Florists' Vade Mecum, The (1683)	Samuel Gilbert
Flower Garden, The (1838)	James M'Intosh
Gardeners' Dictionary, The (1731)	Philip Miller
Hardy Florists Flowers (1880)	James Douglas
Herbal (1596)	John Gerard
Ladies' Companion to the Flower Garden (1845)	Jane Louden
Little English Flora, The (1849)	G. W. Francis
Paradisi in Sole (1629)	John Parkinson
Polyanthus, The (1963)	Roy Genders
Temple of Flora, The (1805)	R. J. Thornton
Vegetable Kingdom, The	John Hill
Wild Flowers (1858)	Spencer Thomson

As the majority of these books are now out of print they are best obtained through libraries or antiquarian booksellers.

Acknowledgements

I would like to thank Doris Gatling for the preparation and typing of this manuscript and John Gledhill for the photographs which are of his consistently high quality. My thanks are also due to my editor, Emma Wood, whose valuable suggestions have been much appreciated. The water colour drawings painted by Mrs Mary McMurtrie are, I think, of the same high quality as those of the botanical artists of the past.

Index